0

The Complete Beginner's Guide to Bowling

The Complete Beginner's Guide to

BOWLING

EDWARD F. DOLAN, JR.

Doubleday & Company, Inc., Garden City, New York   1974

11,440

ISBN: 0-385-01667-0 Trade
0-385-08156-1 Prebound
Library of Congress Catalog Card Number 73–15335
Copyright © 1974 by Edward F. Dolan, Jr.
All Rights Reserved
Printed in the United States of America
First Edition

This book is for my favorite bowlers—WENDY and SHARON

Acknowledgments

For much fine assistance and cooperation in the preparation of this book, I am much in the debt of: the American Bowling Congress; the Woman's International Bowling Congress; Richard Nave and Paul Panholzer of the Nave Lanes, Marin County, California; Mrs. Lorraine Royse of San Rafael, California; James and Florence Stewart of Novato, California; and Richard Lyttle of Inverness, California.

Contents

The Complete Beginner's Guide to Bowling

1. Let's Bowl

Can you pick up a rubber or plastic ball weighing no more than sixteen pounds? Can you then walk with it in a straight line for four steps? And can you swing your arm in an easy pendulum arc as you walk?

If so, you can bowl.

Indeed you can—and, in doing so, you may find your own solution to a problem that bothers countless young Americans. You can get off the sports sidelines.

Are you sitting there now just because you've never been able to find a sport that "fits" you? As a boy, are you too light for football, too short for basketball, or without the right batting eye and throwing arm for baseball? As boy or girl, are you too heavy for competitive swimming, too slow for track, or not quite limber enough for gymnastics?

Or perhaps you haven't been able to find a game that you like. Batting a tennis ball back and forth, throwing a basketball at a hoop, or chasing after a golf ball for eighteen holes just may not be your idea of a good time. Or is it that the sport you would like best is out of the question? Who can surf when the nearest breakers are several hundred—or several thousand—miles away? Who can go out for the water polo, lacrosse, or hockey team when his school doesn't have one?

Whatever your reason, there you are, trapped on the sidelines. Well, why not give bowling a try? You will join about forty million Americans of all ages who love the game and play it regularly, not to mention the estimated one million newcomers who swell its ranks every year. Of the total players, more than fourteen million are nineteen years of age or younger. You will find yourself caught up in an enthusiastic movement that has made bowling the country's second most popular sport, said to be surpassed only by hunting and fishing (and many bowlers will give you an argument about *that*).

And what if you are an athlete who excels in one or more sports? What do you do when your sport is out of season? You know what it is like to be a quarterback in the summer. A skier without snow. A pitcher when the end of school cuts off play at midseason.

Again, there is bowling. Though several forms of the game are played in various parts of the country, the chief type is *tenpins*. It is exclusively an indoor game. It can be played in any season. In any weather. On any day. And at any hour, for many bowling centers are open on a twenty-four-hour basis.

Even if you suffer the difficulty of a physical handicap, bowling may be just the game for you. It has long been enjoyed by wheelchair patients, some of whom have their own leagues. A number of people with but one arm have learned to play. Even the blind participate. Once they are lined up on the pins, they are able to roll a successful ball, for so much of the sport depends simply on the proper action of the arm, wrist, and hand.

Bowling appeals to its forty million players and attracts so many newcomers each year for a variety of reasons. First, it can be played by anyone—man, woman, boy, or girl—of practically any age. At one end of the scale, special lightweight balls are now manufactured so that very young children can get in on the fun. At the other end, the game has a fair share of players in their seventies and eighties. In fact, many centers feature league play for senior citizens.

Second, it is a simple and gentle sport. There is neither the hard body contact of football nor the painful falls of skiing. The whole idea is to roll a ball at ten wooden pins and knock down more of their number than does your opponent. But make no mistake. It's not *all* that simple. It's far more challenging than it seems at first glance. It requires accuracy. Coordination. Concentration. Consistency. In all, it demands a skill that, as it develops, brings great pride and satisfaction.

Finally, bowling is a game for people of all sizes. To excel, you don't have to be basketball's beanpole or football's giant. Boy or girl, you can be tall, short, slender (or plain skinny), chubby, compact, or loose jointed. Size just doesn't matter. You can become an expert bowler.

As a case in point, take the experience of Frank Clause, long a top professional and one of the best bowling instructors in the country. In his book, *How to Win at Bowling*, he recalls that he was a pretty frustrated fellow when a freshman in college. He wanted to go out for sports, but, standing only an inch over five feet, he was too small for football or basketball. He became a cheerleader for a time, but that didn't satisfy him, and so he at last turned to bowling. The rest is history. Frank adds that, right from the start, he enjoyed the game to the fullest and that it filled a great physical and psychological need for him.

Who knows? You may be another Frank Clause—or another petite Judy Audsley, who began bowling at five years of age and went on to become one of the greats in the game. And even if not, you may certainly find a source of lifelong enjoyment.

Well, how about it? Do you think you would like to give bowling a try? If so, you will join in a sport that is not only one of the world's most popular, but also one of its oldest. It can trace its history back to a boy's tomb in the Egypt of seven thousand years ago. Archaeologists came upon the tomb late in the nineteenth century and found several ball-like rocks and pointed stones buried with the child. They were, obviously, the implements of a favorite game that he was taking to the hereafter. And, just as obviously, the rocks were meant to be bowled or thrown at the stones. Archaeologists have set the date of the youngster's burial at about 5200 B.C.

Further, it is known that the ancient Polynesians took pleasure in a bowling game. Called *Ula Maika*, it required them to pelt a target with small elliptically shaped balls and was intended to help them sharpen their hunting eye. Incidentally, the distance between the Polynesian "bowler" of old and his target was sixty feet—the exact same length as today's bowling lane.

The kind of bowling that we now play comes from Europe and appears to have gotten its start as a religious ritual for German churchgoers in around A.D. 300. It seems that the peasants of the day always carried war clubs for protection, taking them even into church. There, the priests tried to make the idea of Satan very real for their parishioners and so developed a ritual in which each peasant stood his club in a corner and then rolled a large rock or ball at it. The club represented the devil and, if the peasant managed to knock it over, he earned a smile and the word that he was obviously a good and virtuous man. But if he missed, he was told that he needed to live a better life.

Incidentally, the war clubs were called *kegels*. To this day, bowling is still known as *kegling*, and bowlers are still nicknamed *keglers*.

Bowling did not long remain just a religious ceremony, for people quickly saw the good fun that was to be had in trying to knock over the clubs. A sport was born, one whose popularity spread rapidly throughout Germany. It soon became a regular feature of village celebrations and family get-togethers. Wealthy landowners bowled on the lawns of their estates. Townspeople set up areas for the game behind local taverns, in their yards, and in village squares. By the Middle Ages, bowling had moved on to the Netherlands, France, Italy, and the Scandinavian countries, soon thereafter leaping the English Channel to England and Scotland.

Popular though it was, the infant game was anything but a well-organized one with the same set of rules and equipment for all. It was played the way that any group of people in any country wanted to play it, though the basic idea was always to hit or to come as close as possible to a target with a rolled ball. In some areas, sticks that were soon called *pins* replaced the first kegels. In other spots, balls smaller than those rolled by the bowler served for the kegels. Eventually, in all but just a few forms of bowling, the pins won out as targets. But there was no uniformity so far as their size and number were concerned. Some were large. Some were small. Some games used as few as three pins, while some others called for as many as fifteen. Nor, aside from being round, was there much similarity among the balls. They, too, could be large or small. They could be made of wood or iron. Or they could be carefully smoothed and polished rocks.

Just as varied were the types of bowling games that took shape throughout Europe. *Bowls,* a game in which a ball is rolled along the grass toward a smaller target ball, flourished in several countries and became especially popular in England. Now, more than eight hundred years later, it is still played in England, Canada, Australia, and New Zealand; it is also enjoyed in several eastern areas of the United States, where it is usually called *lawn bowls.* A similar game, *boccie,* was—and still is—an Italian favorite. Liked by the Irish was *road bowling,* which called for contestants to roll stones along a roadway from village to village. Scotland, a land of bitter winters, first took *curling* to its heart in the sixteenth century and has kept it there ever since. A form of bowling that is played on ice, curling requires its players to send a polished, disclike stone sliding toward a circular mark more than a hundred feet away. Exactly where the game was born is unknown (some historians believe that it originated in the Netherlands), but Scotland was the first country in which it found widespread popularity. Today, it is played not only there, but in such other nations as Canada, Germany, Switzerland, Norway, Sweden, and the United States. In fact, wherever the winters are icy, there you will likely find curling.

Of all the variations, the game that finally won the greatest popularity and became the father of today's sport was *kegelspiel,* which was first played in Germany and the Netherlands. In it, a player rolled a ball along a narrow path, aiming it at a collection of wooden pins that were set up in the shape of a diamond, the idea being to topple all the pins except the one in the center. The first paths varied in length and were built on beds of clay or cinders, but eventually a length of sixty feet was made standard, and a wooden board about a foot wide was set down on the path and the ball was rolled along it. The number of pins used ranged from nine to fifteen for many years. In the sixteenth century, the great religious leader, Martin Luther, himself an ardent "kegler," established nine as the official number for the game. Soon thereafter, kegel-spiel became known in English as *ninepins*.

The Dutch are credited with bringing bowling to America in the 1600s. They established an area for the game in New York City, giving it the name by which it is still called: Bowling Green.

Ninepins was enjoyed as much here as in Europe, even winning a place for itself in American literature. In Washington Irving's story of Rip Van Winkle, a sound that seems to be distant thunder turns out not to be thunder at all but the crash of balls hitting their targets in a game of ninepins being played by elfin Dutchmen.

As the country grew, ninepins grew with it, moving steadily westward. By the mid-1800s, both outdoor and indoor lanes (the British, incidentally, are said to be the inventors of the indoor lane, reportedly establishing the first one in London in the mid-1400s) were to be found in most large cities and in many small towns. But, at the very same time, ninepins fell on bad days. Men began to bet heavily on the outcome of games, and very soon the sport was taken over by cheats and professional gamblers. They gave ninepins a reputation so unsavory that the states of Connecticut and New York finally passed laws forbidding its play.

Thanks to those laws, the sport of bowling as we play it today was born. The laws referred strictly to ninepins, and some bowling alley owners immediately sidestepped them and remained in business simply by adding a tenth pin to the game. In so doing, they invented tenpins. The newcomer pin made necessary a revision in the pin setup. The old diamond shape disappeared and was replaced by the now familiar triangular arrangement.

For a long while, however, tenpins had to suffer the same poor reputation endured by ninepins. Much gambling still plagued the game and, even when it finally lost its hold, people were slow to forget it. They looked on bowling alleys as the smoky haunts of hoodlums. Families who might well have wanted to play tenpins stayed safely away. Children were forbidden to pause outside or even to pass close by. Women feared to go near even the lanes that were known to be respectable and properly operated. If some could not overcome the temptation to try the game, they had to sneak in the back door or risk disgrace. Then the proprietor would protect them from view by shielding their playing area with a canvas screen.

There were a number of people, however, who saw bowling as a fine game that deserved a better reputation. Twice in the late nineteenth century, they tried to form associations that would govern the game and clear its name of all taint. They failed on both occasions, but a third attempt succeeded. In September 1895, a group made up of players, bowling alley owners, and manufacturers of bowling equipment met in New York City and founded the American Bowling Congress.

Primarily, the ABC wanted to promote the sport and give it a new and deserved respectability. Additionally, it sought to adopt uniform rules and regulations so that, wherever it was played, bowling would be the same, with the competition always fair and equal for all participants.

That the ABC achieved its aims is seen in the fact that it remains today a chief governing agency in bowling. Tenpins is played throughout the country according to the rules that the ABC long ago established. Bowling centers everywhere construct and maintain their equipment and facilities according to its specifications and standards. The organization administers bowling's Hall of Fame, sponsors the oldest and biggest annual bowling tournament in the nation, and sends American players to international competitions.

The ABC, whose membership is male, was in time joined by other organizations, all of whom work to promote bowling as a wholesome and exciting sport. In 1916, the Woman's International Bowling Congress was formed to foster participation by women and to sponsor league play and tournaments for them. It began with a membership of about forty and has grown until its members now number about three million; they participate in more than 121,000 WIBC-sanctioned leagues in upward of three thousand American cities and in several foreign countries. Later, the American Junior Bowling Congress came into being for young people up to eighteen years of age. Administered by the ABC, it sponsors league play, tournaments, and instructional programs for close to four hundred thousand junior players.

In addition, the sport is served by the Bowling Proprietors Association of America, the Professional Bowlers Association, the Professional Women's Bowlers Association, and the National Bowling Council. One of the principal activities of this last organization is the bowling program that it conducts to help in the rehabilitation of hospitalized and blind war veterans.

Bowling's popularity grew slowly during the first years of this century and then swelled immeasurably after World War II. Countless young service people, men and women alike, learned the game in the recreation centers at military bases during the war and brought it home with them. It, too, was a favorite with wartime workers, who, because of gasoline rationing, could not travel far for recreation; they continued to play after hostilities ended. The enthusiasm of all was infectious. Interest in the sport spread far and wide.

Helping matters along were the bowling proprietors. With but few exceptions, the bowling alleys of earlier years had been small and dimly lighted places, often located in basements. Now the owners replaced them with bright and modern centers, rounding them out with such inviting facilities as coffee shops, restaurants, soft-drink counters, pro shops for the purchase of equipment, and baby-sitting services for parents. Further, they won countless new customers by establishing leagues for team play. Into existence came daytime leagues for housewives; evening leagues for men, women, social groups, and business firms; and afternoon and weekend leagues for young people.

Finally, in the 1950s, the proprietors installed the newly developed automatic pinsetter—and what a boon it proved to be. Hitherto, pins had always been set by pinboys—young men who usually did the job to earn after-school money. Few centers were ever able to find and hire enough to go around, and many a customer had to be turned away just because there was no one there to take care of the pins for him. The automatic pinsetter ended the problem. It collected the fallen pins, swept those away that were left lying on the lane, and returned them all to their triangular arrangement. Won back were the turned-away customers. Now a person could play at any time of the day or night and not give a thought to reassembling the pins.

It is in a modern, well-lighted center, complete with all its varied services and automatic pinsetters, that you will learn to bowl. Let's go there now and get started. Let's walk past the restaurant, the soft-drink counter, and the pro shop. Let's get right to the playing area and do what any top-notch athlete in any sport first does.

Let's get to know your "playing field" and your equipment.

2. Welcome to the Lanes

The playing area in any bowling center is divided into a series of wooden lanes, all identical. In most centers, the lanes number from twenty-four to thirty-six, though some rural spots have as few as a dozen, while certain big-city and suburban locations boast of more than sixty. They are built in pairs, with each pair split down its length by a covered track along which the ball is returned to a holding rack after each roll. This arrangement is used to conserve space by allowing two separate groups of players to use the same return unit.

Long ago, when the ABC set up uniform regulations for the game, it also established firm specifications governing the measurements and the construction of all lanes and the equipment that goes with them. Every reputable center today adheres to these specifications. Thanks to them, you can begin your play in California and then move to Florida without worrying about a single bowling change. The lanes, the ball, the pins, and the scoring—all will be the same.

THE LANE

Your first look at a lane will show you that it actually consists of several parts, of which the lane itself is but one. At its one end is the approach area, at its other the pin deck, and along its side nine-inch-wide gutters that catch misdirected balls. The lane is separated from the approach area by the foul line. In the distance, the pin deck stands in front of the cushioned, boxlike pit into which the ball and toppled pins fall.

Situated behind the pin deck and extending out and over it is the automatic pinsetter. In most centers, its upper machinery is hidden from player view by a wall that is variously called the *pinvisor* or *pindicator*. It is an electrically powered, glassed-in screen that, flashing an illuminated diagram of the pin arrangement, signals the player of the pins left in place after a roll. You will find it particularly helpful when you leave one pin standing directly behind another and run the risk of not seeing it from a distance. Some pindicators flash an arrow on

the spot in the diagram that constitutes your best target for downing the remaining pins.

The lane itself extends 60 feet from the foul line to the center of the first pin—called the *headpin*—and then another 2 feet, 10³⁄₁₆ inches to the pit. It is 41 to 42 inches wide and is constructed of maple and pine planks, with the former stretching away from the foul line for 15 feet, and the latter then taking over to run to the pindeck, where maple is again found. The maple planks, expensive and tough, are used ahead of the pine because they are capable of withstanding the punishment of thrown balls. Once the ball is rolling smoothly, the less expensive pine is capable of handling it.

All the planks are set on their narrow sides and are about an inch wide. When first installed, they are fastened tightly together, are sanded smooth and flat, and are given a durable glasslike surface with several coats of lacquer. Embedded into the lane at that time are two sets of markers. One, located seven feet out from the foul line, is a series of ten dots, or dowels. Nine feet farther along is a triangular arrangement of seven arrows, called *range finders*. Both sets, as you will see later, are intended to help you target in on the pins.

The lane floor must be as flat as it is humanly possible to make it. ABC specifications dictate that its level must not vary more than 40/1,000 inch in any spot. Since continued use is bound to dent and groove any lane, the ABC periodically inspects the level. Further, the ABC requires that a lane be resanded and relacquered at least once in every two-year period.

THE PINS

Up on the pin deck, the triangular pin arrangement measures thirty-six inches along each of its sides. The pins are placed so that there is a spacing of twelve inches from the center of one to the center of another. They are numbered from 1 to 10, as shown in the illustration.

The numbers are intended for pin identification only. They have nothing to do with scoring. Scoring is based on the total

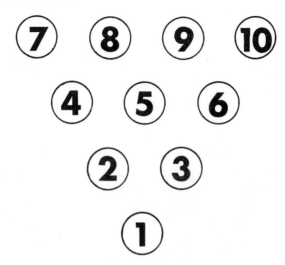

pins toppled and not on their number designations. For instance, were you to knock over the 1 and 2 pins, your tally would not be 3, but 2.

Each pin, which is bottle-shaped and still has something of the old war club look to it, is built of hard, laminated rock maple. Covered over with a strong plastic coating, it stands 15 inches high. Its diameters vary—from $2^{16}/_{24}$ inches at the base to $4^{49}/_{64}$ inches at the belly and $1^{43}/_{64}$ inches at the neck.

A pin may weigh from 2 pounds 14 ounces to 3 pounds 10 ounces. In a set of 10, however, the weight of one pin cannot vary more than 4 ounces from that of another.

THE BOWLING BALL

In days gone by, bowling balls were fashioned of rock, wood, or iron. Today, each is manufactured of either hard rubber or plastic.

The modern bowling ball must measure no more than twenty-seven inches in circumference. At maximum, it weighs sixteen pounds, but its weight may descend to lows of eight and ten pounds. It is built with cork at its center, with its weight much determined by the amount of cork used.

Ball weights vary so that all players can bowl with ease. Men and older boys generally use sixteen-pounders, while women and younger people usually turn to those in the twelve-to-fifteen-pound range. Ten-pound balls are made for children, and eight-pounders for the very young who want to get an earlier-than-usual start at the game.

All talk of ball weight here, however, must be general. Weight is a matter of personal preference, depending much on a bowler's strength (as opposed to poundage) and his coordination. Some lightweight players can easily handle a sixteen-pounder, while some heavyweights can't roll a good score with it no matter how they try. It is a subject that we will go into more thoroughly in the next chapter.

Today's ball is customarily drilled with three fingerholes: one for the thumb, the others for the middle and ring fingers. The thumbhole is located singly, while its companions are set as a pair. Depending on hand size, the two fingerholes are drilled at varying distances from the thumbhole and from each other.

THE APPROACH AREA

It is from the approach area that balls are rolled to the pins. As wide as the lane, it extends sixteen feet back from the foul line, affording any player sufficient room for the steps needed to carry him through the armswing that sends the ball on its way.

Embedded in its floor are three rows of dots, or dowels. One row lies fifteen feet back from the foul line, the second twelve feet back, and the third just two inches back. There are seven dots in the foul line row and five each in the two rear rows. Like the dowels and range finders out in the lane, their purpose is to help in aiming.

When you ready yourself to bowl, you stand by the dot of your choice in one of the rear rows and then advance through the armswing to an appropriate one in the foul line row. In so doing, you make certain that you move along a path proper for your target. And, in so doing time and again, you always bowl in the same way, assuring your game the consistency that is required for the best scores.

The rear rows are placed at distances estimated to bring you right up to the foul line as you complete your armswing and release the ball. Your feet must never cross the foul line, for such encroachment on the lane cancels your count for the roll. The fifteen-foot line is positioned with men and older boys in mind, while the twelve-foot line is intended for women, younger bowlers, and shorter players. But again, as in ball weights, these are generalizations. Many a bowler—just as you may do—finds that his best starting position is somewhere in front of or between the two rows.

To the rear of the approach area are seats for the players. Off to the side is the scoring table. The table is often equipped with an overhead projector that casts an image of the score sheet on a screen above. The projector is used principally in league play so that the spectators can keep tabs on the various team counts.

Mention of the table brings us to a subject that confuses many a beginner: the scoring in bowling. You've undoubtedly heard that it is difficult and mystifying, and, indeed, it does seem complex at first glance. But there is no reason why it should bother you for more than a few minutes; for underneath it all, it is really a simple matter.

Let's prove the point right now.

SCORING

You need know, first, that a game consists of ten *frames*, with a frame being to bowling what an inning is to baseball. You are allowed to bowl twice in each frame unless you manage to knock down all the pins on your first roll. You earn a point for each pin toppled and, in addition, you give yourself bonuses—or rewards—for certain good hits that we will talk about in a moment. You record your points on a score sheet provided by the center.

The score sheet is divided into lines, one line per player per game. In its turn, each line is divided into ten boxes, one to a frame. In common with the game's "innings," the boxes are called frames. Your score, which is cumulative, is placed in them as you go along.

When you take your first look at a score sheet, you will see that each frame has a small square located in its upper right-hand corner. Into these squares go marks representing the types of rolls, both good and bad, that you make during the game. Together, your score and the marks provide you with a complete record of your performance. At game's end, the score

will show you how well you did or did not do, and the marks will show you why. They will indicate where you performed well and where you ran into problems.

In all, you will need to learn six marks. They represent the following triumphs and headaches:

1. *Strike:* This is your best shot of all. With it, you topple all the pins on your first roll in the frame. Trot happily back to the score sheet and mark the square in the appropriate frame with an *X*.

2. *Spare:* The spare is your "second best" shot. All the pins go down in two rolls. Mark the proper square with a diagonal line.

3. *Miss:* This one is a disappointment. It means that you fail to knock down all the pins in two rolls. A dash goes into the square.

4. *Split:* Here, with your first roll, you leave two or more pins upright with spaces between them where other pins had been standing. On your second roll, you are unable to clear them all away, and so into the square goes a circle. Some splits can mean real trouble: for instance, the 7-10 variety, in which the standing pins are clear across the lane from each other. Short

of a miracle, you're not going to be able to get both with your second roll. Others, fortunately, aren't too hard to handle.

5. *Converted split:* With this one, you can be happy again. It means that you turn a split—"convert it" is the bowler's term—into a spare on your second roll. Breathe a sigh of relief and put a circle with a diagonal line through it in the square.

6. *Foul:* As you know, when you step beyond the foul line in rolling your ball, you commit a foul. Unhappily, you lose your points for the roll, a particular tragedy if you bowl a strike. Indicate the foul by writing the letter *F* in the square.

It was mentioned earlier that certain of your rolls will earn you bonus points during the game. Those rolls are the strike and the spare. For the strike, you earn 10 points for the frame, plus the total of pins that you knock over in your next 2 rolls. For the spare, you receive 10 points, with your bonus being the total number of pins toppled on your next roll.

Right here, let's clear up a point that confuses so many beginners. When you roll a strike or a spare, you do not take your bonus shots immediately. You must wait until the next frame before doing so. Consequently, you do not write down your score right away. It goes onto the sheet only after you have completed your bonus rolls.

Using the spare as an example, let's see how this works. Suppose that, in your opening frame, you knock down seven pins on the first roll and three on the second. Though you have earned a count of 10, do not record it on the score sheet yet; rather, just put the diagonal mark in the square as a reminder of what you've done. Next, when it is your turn to bowl in the second frame, let's say that you topple five pins on the first roll. Now you know what your final count for the first frame is going to be—10 for the spare and a bonus of 5 or a total of 15.

One more small point: How do you score the second frame? Let's say that on your second roll, you topple 3 pins. In all, you have 8 pins for the frame. Add that 8 to your 15 total for the first frame. Your second-frame score stands at 23.

But suppose you are really doing fine today. Suppose that, on your final roll in the second frame, you clear away all 5 remaining pins, giving yourself another spare. What do you do? Simple. Again, write down no score, but merely tag the small square with a diagonal line. You've got yourself another 10 points, plus the pins to be downed on your first roll in the third frame. If, say, they turn out to be 4, you will then have a 14 count. You add 14 to your first-frame total of 15. Your score for the second frame is 29.

Now, let's say that you topple only 2 pins on your second roll in the third frame. Altogether for the frame, you have claimed 6 pins. Add 6 to your second-frame total of 29. Your score in the third frame comes to 35.

But, if you again make a spare, you jot down another little diagonal mark and wait until your first roll in the next frame. Repeat the process for as long as you go on bowling spares. The same applies for the strike—except that your bonus is the total of pins toppled on the following 2 rolls.

Incidentally, speaking of strikes, the maximum number of points that you can make with them in any frame is 30. For this reason, a perfect game—one in which you roll nothing but strikes—comes exactly to 300.

The best way to learn how to score in bowling is to keep track of an actual game. Since we all can't get together at a center, let's do the next best thing: roll an imaginary game.

Here, to begin with, is your score sheet as it will appear at the end of the game. Shall we see how it got to be that way?

1	2	3	4	5	6	7	8	9	10
—	╱	—	✕	—	✕	✕	✕	—	⊞
7	22	29	48	57	87	112	130	138	147

First Frame

On your first roll, you topple 5 pins. Down go 2 more on your second roll, for a tally of 7. Mark your total in the first frame on the score sheet. Place a dash in the small square.

Second Frame

Your game improves a little, for over go nine pins on the first roll. You clear away the remaining one on the second roll, recording a spare. You have earned 10 points, and you have bonus points coming up on the first roll in the next frame. Mark the square in the second-frame box with a diagonal line.

Third Frame

With your first ball, you knock over 5 pins. Now it's time to record your second-frame score. Add 5 pins to your 10 for the spare, for a 15 count. Then add the 15 to your first-frame total of 7. Your second-frame score is 22.

You now roll your second ball. Down go two pins. Your total for the third frame knockdowns is 7. Add this to your 22 in the second frame, giving you a third-frame score of 29. Put a dash in the small square.

Fourth Frame

Wow! Your first ball is perfectly rolled. There is a clatter of pins, and all are cleared away for a strike. You have earned 10 points, plus a bonus of the pins toppled on your next 2 rolls. Do not record any score as yet. Just place the X in the small square.

Fifth Frame

Your first ball topples 7 pins, and your second 2 pins, earning a tally of 9. To bring your fourth-frame score up to date, add your 10 points for the strike to the 9 pins just downed, for a count of 19. Add 19 to your third-frame total of 29. Your score for the fourth frame is 48. Now, to finish things off, add your 9 pins in frame five to your 48 total. Your score at the end of the fifth frame is 57. Put a dash in the small square.

Sixth Frame

Wow again! You register another strike. Put the X in the small square for the sixth frame, but do not write in any score. Wait until you have finished your next 2 rolls.

Seventh Frame

You do it again! Another strike! Two in a row. What this is going to do for your score! But you still cannot start to total things up. Remember, you still have some more rolls coming. Put an X in the small square in the seventh-frame box.

Eighth Frame

Oh, oh! What do you know about that! Another strike. Put an X in the small square for the eighth frame and begin to add up your count. You have had 2 rolls since your first strike back there in the sixth frame. You have 10 points for that strike, 10 points for your first roll following it (another strike), and 10 points for your second roll (still another strike), for a count of 30. Add 30 to your total of 57 in the fifth frame. Your score at the end of the sixth frame is 87. For the time being, you can do no more, for you still have further bonus rolls coming.

Ninth Frame

This time, you knock down 5 pins with your first ball. Now, it is time to score for your seventh frame, for you have had two rolls since the strike there. Take 10 points for your seventh-frame strike, 10 for the eighth-frame strike, and 5 for your first roll in the ninth, giving you a count of 25. Add this to your sixth-frame total of 87. Your seventh frame brings you to 112.

Now you roll your second ball. Down go 3 pins. Altogether in the frame, you have toppled 8 pins. At this point, you can bring your scoring up to date, filling in both the eighth- and ninth-frame boxes. For the eighth frame, give yourself 10 points for the strike and 8 points for the next 2 balls rolled. The total is 18, which is added to your 112 score, bringing your count to 130 for the eighth frame. To finish off your figuring, add your eight pins in the ninth frame to the 130 count. Your ninth-frame total comes to 138.

Tenth Frame

Your two rolls topple 9 pins: 5 on the first roll and 4 on the second. You now simply complete your scoring by adding 9 to your 138 total, for a final score of 147.

With your score of 147, you've done very well for yourself. It's a total of which you can always be pretty proud.

Now, for just two points in closing.

First, you will notice that the small square in the tenth frame is divided into three sections. This is done to help you keep track of things should you strike or spare in the frame and so earn additional rolls. Incidentally, on some score sheets, you will find that each of the other squares is divided into two small compartments. One compartment is used to record the number of pins toppled on the first roll in a frame, while the other serves for the scoring marks.

Last of all, you need always keep in mind one fact about tenth-frame strikes and spares. You are allowed only two bonus rolls for the final frame and no more. Suppose that you roll strikes on your bonus rolls. Ordinarily, you would be able to go on bowling so that you could add up the totals for the subsequent hits. Not so in the tenth frame. You have a maximum of two bonus rolls, regardless of what they are.

3. Your Equipment

Those of you who play golf know that a good set of clubs can easily cost more than $200. Those who have tried their hand at sailing need not be told how much money and time can disappear into the upkeep of even the smallest boat. And those who cycle will tell you that a quality ten-speed runs between $100 and $150 new and that, unless you make a lucky buy, you cannot get a used model for much less.

But what of bowling? Not only is it a sport that can be played in any weather or season, but it is also one of the most economical. Its basic items of equipment—ball, tote bag, and shoes—are just about as inexpensive to purchase as any sports gear you care to mention. Nor, aside from the shoes, is any special clothing needed. Your good old comfortable leisure-time wear will ordinarily do quite nicely. In all, though you may want to buy more expensive equipment as you become a better player, you can outfit yourself for a long while in bowling with an investment of as little as $30 to $35.

Too, you need not immediately purchase any equipment. In fact, you should *not* make a single purchase right away, but should first give yourself a chance to learn the game and find out if it's really "the one for you." Then you can feel free to break into your savings account and head for the sports shop.

In the meantime, you can use the equipment provided by the bowling center.

In using the center's equipment or in buying your own, there are certain facts that you need know about the basic "tools" of bowling. These facts will not guarantee you a strike on every roll. But they *will* play an important part in helping you master the game.

Let's look at them now.

THE BALL

It goes without saying that the ball is the most important single piece of player equipment in bowling. Right from the start, it can make or break your game. Aside from a clean strike, there is nothing more pleasing to a bowler than a ball that he is able to grasp comfortably and release smoothly and easily. But nothing is worse than a loose-fitting one that seems ready to fly out of his hand on the backswing, or one with fingerholes so tight that it promises to drag him down the lane behind it.

When you are first bowling and using balls provided by the center (they are customarily called "house balls" and are available without charge), you should take care to find one that pleases you and seems easy to handle. *Patience* must be your key word here. Take your time as you search among the racks where the balls are stored. Do not settle on the first ball that you see. Check several and compare them before making your choice. Look for the one that has the best *weight*, the most comfortable *fingerholes*, and the proper *span*.

Ball Weight

As you know, ball weights range from a minimum of eight pounds to a maximum of sixteen. The basic rule for selecting a ball of proper weight is to choose *the heaviest one that you can deliver without undue strain.*

When a ball rolls into its target, it topples several of the pins and, as they go down, they "mix" with the surrounding pins and topple them. You want the heaviest ball possible, for the weightier it is, the more power it can gather to give you a good mix. But bowling is not all power. Far more important is accuracy. And so avoid getting too ambitious. Do not pick a ball that is too heavy, for it will prove difficult to swing and will tire your arm and hand quickly, thus canceling out your accuracy. The heaviest ball that you can deliver without undue strain will put both accuracy and weight on your side.

On the other hand, do not make the mistake of choosing a too-light ball, thinking that you will be easily able to put some extra power and speed into its roll. True, you will get much speed and power, but the chances are that you will send the ball sailing through the pins so fast that it will not help them come up with a good mix. Too, because you seem to have so little weight at hand, you will also probably be tempted to "rush the foul line"—that is, to hurry your armswing and thus lose the steady rhythm that is so vital for a good roll.

The selection of a suitably heavy ball is chiefly a matter of trial and error. You will need to try a number of experimental swings with a variety of balls before you make your choice. As you experiment, ask yourself: Am I in control of the swing? Does the ball put too much strain on my arm and hand? Or is it so light that I find myself "whipping" it along? Sooner or later, the answers to these questions will point out the right ball weight for you.

Once you have learned that weight, keep it in mind so that you will not waste time in rechecking for it when next you play. Most house balls are stamped with their weights. In some centers, the weights are number coded. If you do not know what a coded number stands for, ask the personnel at the center.

Fingerholes

Though models with two fingerholes were once fashionable, practically all bowling balls today are drilled with three fingerholes—for the thumb, the middle finger, and the ring finger. When searching for a properly fitting house ball, check the thumbhole first. It should fit loosely, but should not be so roomy as to allow you to double-up your thumb even to the least degree. Too, it should be deep enough to accept your thumb to the full length. Once you have inserted your thumb, rotate it several times. The fit is proper if you can feel just the slightest friction.

The holes for your middle and ring fingers, though they should not be too tight, need to fit a little more snugly than the thumbhole. When you have inserted the two fingers, you should be able to feel some friction between them and the sides of the holes.

The thumbhole must fit somewhat loosely because, as you will see in the next chapter, your thumb is the first to come away when you release the ball to the pins, and it must do so easily and smoothly. Your fingers, for their part, remain behind for a split second and must then lift the ball slightly to give it direction and spin. Unless their holes are a bit on the snug side, your fingers will lose their grip before they can do the work assigned them.

Span

The *span* is the distance across the surface of the ball from the thumbhole to each of the fingerholes. Proper span is quite as vital to your game as are correct weight and fingerhole sizes. A ball with too narrow a span will cramp your fingers, while one with too wide a span will weaken them by spreading them too wide. In either case, your hand will quickly tire and the ball will seem to weigh as much as *twice* its actual weight. And then out the window will go your accuracy.

There is nothing mysterious about finding a ball with the span right for you. Just use this simple test. Insert your thumb the full distance into the thumbhole and then spread your middle and ring fingers out over the holes meant for them. If the middle knuckle of each finger falls directly over its hole, you've found the right span.

And, if you wish to go a step farther, try the pencil test. Once your thumb and fingers are in place, slide the pencil back and forth between your palm and the surface of the ball. You should have just enough room to do so.

PURCHASING A BOWLING BALL

Although it is well and fine to begin your bowling career with a house ball, you should attempt to purchase a ball of your own as soon as you have the knack of the game. Only with your own ball can you be assured that you have exactly the right one for the size of your fingers and the span of your hand.

All experienced bowlers say that a ball should fit the player "like a glove." You cannot hope to get a "glove fit" with a house ball. The house ball must be a friendly thing that can get along with as many bowlers as possible, and so its finger-holes are spaced and drilled to fit the average hand and to be used by either right- or left-handers. The house ball may well serve an army of bowlers, but only by accident will it ever serve any one of them perfectly.

Bowling balls may be purchased at the bowling center or a sports shop. They usually run around twenty dollars to more than fifty dollars, with the most expensive models coming in brightly colored plastic. Each ball arrives "blank" from the manufacturer, meaning that it is without fingerholes. Its retail price customarily includes the cost of drilling the fingerholes.

When you make your purchase, the dealer will first discuss the matter of weight with you and help you make the best choice possible. Next, using a special measuring device, he will determine your exact hand span and the size of your thumb and fingers so that properly fitting fingerholes can be drilled. He will work slowly and carefully to get a good fit. Then he will either drill the holes himself or turn the job over to that treasured bowling specialist, the expert ball driller.

The dealer may not concentrate on just finger size and hand span when getting ready to drill the holes. Under discussion also may come the matter of *pitch*. Pitch is the often-heard term that confuses many a novice bowler. It means the angle at which the fingerholes are bored into the ball. These angles help you to release and to lift the ball with ease.

Most house balls have what is called a three-eighths inch inward pitch, which is considered best for the average hand. With this conventional pitch, were a centerline to be drawn from the fingerholes, it would pass through a point three-eighths inch above the centerline.

But your hand may not be within the average range, and so you may need another type of pitch. You may need a *zero* pitch or a *reverse* pitch. A centerline drawn from a zero-pitched fingerhole will pass directly through the center of the ball, while one drawn from a reverse-pitched hole will cut through a point slightly below dead center.

Many dealers will automatically drill the conventional inward pitch unless the customer specifies otherwise. And so, if the dealer fails to bring the matter up, you should be sure to mention it yourself, even though the conventional pitch turns out to be the one best suited for you. Talk over the whole subject of pitch with the dealer. He will help you make the best decision possible.

Now, for some words of warning:

Beware of "bargain" balls that are sometimes placed on sale in department stores and discount shops. In particular, do not try to save a few cents by buying a bargain ball with the holes predrilled. If you do, you are sacrificing every chance of getting that necessary "glove fit." Also, do not allow the store to send the ball off to a vague someone or someplace to have the holes drilled. Make certain that it is drilled by an expert.

And avoid buying your ball from the salesman who strikes you as not knowing what he is talking about or not really caring about the ball he is selling you. You will not likely run into this kind of salesman at a bowling center or in a top-notch sports shop, but he is an all-too-common sight in the large department store or discount house that assigns its personnel to counters on the basis of need and not knowledge or interest. In particular, do not let a salesman measure you for a ball if he stares blankly at the measuring device as if it has just arrived from outer space. If you must buy a ball from him, carry it out and have it measured and drilled by someone who knows what he's doing. Your best bet, however, is to say a polite "Thank you" and make your purchase elsewhere.

Oddly enough, even when the ball has been expertly drilled, you may find it a little clumsy to work with at first. This is simply because you are unfamiliar with it, so give it a chance, even though your scores tumble for a time. You will need a few days of practice before your game is back to normal.

Too, even with an expert drilling job, you may find that the fingerholes are still not exactly the right size. If they are a little on the tight side, the dealer can enlarge them. And should they prove too large (though this rarely happens with good measuring and drilling), he can "plug" them with liquid plastic. After it has hardened, he will drill a new set of holes.

Sometimes you will find that the edges of the holes are sharp and chafe your fingers. The dealer can easily bevel the edges, or you can often take care of the problem yourself with a bit of sandpaper. Chafed fingers are also a sign of improperly fitted holes. The size of the holes, of course, should be immediately checked and revised accordingly.

Surely, nothing needs be said about the care you must give to the upkeep of your ball. It should be cleaned during and after every bowling session so that it doesn't spend its life coated with lane grit; you can clean it with a rag or with the buffing machines found at every center. And it should be kept away from temperature extremes, for its composition can be damaged by severe heat or cold.

When you purchase your bowling ball, you should also buy a tote bag for it. The bag will protect the ball and will obviously make it easier for you to carry from home to the lanes. Tote bags come in a variety of materials, ranging from canvas and plastic to fancy-tooled leather. Less expensive bags can be purchased for under five dollars. The most expensive models cost as much as fifty dollars or more.

SHOES

You must wear special shoes when bowling. They are constructed with a leather sole on one shoe and a rubber sole on the other.

Why?

You can easily answer that question by trying to deliver a ball while wearing just leather-soled shoes or tennis sneakers. The approach surface, while not slippery, is slick, and leather-soled shoes will cause you to slide too much as you release the ball, at the least ruining your aim, and at the worst sending your feet out from under you.

One foot, however, needs to slide a little as you deliver the ball. Tennis sneakers will permit no slide at all. They will only serve as brakes, with the result that you may lose your balance or stumble forward, perhaps sending your ball into the gutter and perhaps giving your muscles a painful wrench.

With regulation bowling shoes, the leather sole gives you your needed slide, while the rubber sole provides the traction necessary to move you forward into your armswing and then acts as a brake to slow you down at the end of the swing. For a reason you will see in the next chapter, the leather sole will be on the left shoe if you are a right-handed bowler, and on the opposite shoe if you are a left-hander. The heels are made of rubber so that they will not mark the approach floor and will assist in the braking action. The tip of the leather sole is likewise made of rubber; it, too, joins in the braking action.

All bowling centers carry a stock of bowling shoes and will rent out pairs to customers, with the rental cost usually running around twenty-five cents. For your first sessions, you can easily manage with "house shoes," but you should soon purchase a pair of your own.

You will want your own pair, first, for obvious hygienic reasons. And, of course, shoes of your own will give you the best fit and thus help your game. Although the center may carry shoes in practically every size, it may not be able to give you an exact fit. Just as an ill-fitting ball will hinder your game, so will shoes that are too tight or too loose. You simply cannot fully enjoy yourself—or hope to roll a high score—if your feet are uncomfortable.

Bowling shoes are made of soft leather and are manufactured in a variety of styles and colors. They can be purchased from a low of about $7.50 to highs of $20 and $25. You will do well to start with an inexpensive pair and then graduate to a better quality as you grow more expert.

You may, if you wish, purchase your shoes and bowling bag in matching colors. You may also buy a small bag for just your shoes. It will usually cost less than $5.

Once you have bought your bowling shoes, never wear them for any purpose but bowling. And wait until you arrive at the center before putting them on. Do not wear them from home. Otherwise, dirt and grime will collect on the soles and interfere with their sliding and braking abilities. Too—and this will do anything but endear you to the heart of the bowling proprietor—they will streak and mar the approach area.

A final tip from the experts: Develop the habit of checking your soles whenever you return to the approach area from any other part of the center. Suppose that you have gone to the soft-drink stand or the water fountain. If you have accidentally stepped in some water, it will cancel out the slide in your leather sole and turn it into a brake.

CLOTHING

As was said earlier, your regular leisure-time wear will likely be all that you need in the way of bowling clothes, although (especially if you are a girl) you may find it difficult to pass up some of the stylish lane togs found today in all sports shops. Bowling instructors customarily advise slacks and a shirt, T-shirt, or pullover sweater for boys, and a skirt or slacks along with a blouse or pullover sweater for girls.

A word of caution, however, is necessary. Your clothing should be comfortable, should allow you complete freedom of movement, and should never interfere with your armswing and delivery. Any outfit that gets in your way—no matter how cherished and "in" it may be—is not for bowling.

Very tight slacks, skirts, and jeans, for example, should be avoided, for they will bind you throughout your approach steps and especially as you stretch forward to release the ball. Shirts and blouses should not be allowed to hang out and brush your arm during its swing; for the same reason, flared skirts and baggy sweaters should be left at home. Left there with them, too, should be short skirts. All too often, they cause the player to restrict her movements in an effort to preserve her modesty.

SPECIAL ACCESSORIES

Practically all sports shops and many bowling centers carry special player accessories. Such equipment ranges from leather straps that hold the wrist firm to gloves and creams that promise a more secure grip on the ball. Though some may eventually prove helpful to your game, you can safely pass them all by in your beginning days—and perhaps for as long as you play. Not a one is really necessary for good bowling. Ball, shoes, tote bag, and comfortable clothing are the essentials. In addition to them, you need only a love for the sport and a willingness to work for the concentration and accuracy that it requires.

Thus far, we have seen how the game is played and scored. We have seen the equipment necessary to get you started. Now, let's pick out a lane and get to work.

It's time to bowl.

4. The Fundamentals: That Easy Pendulum Swing

Simple though it is in concept, bowling makes one great demand on every player. That demand is accuracy. Without it, you can send a ball down a lane every minute of the day for the rest of your life and still never come up with a good score.

The need for accuracy, however, should not discourage you. There is nothing magical about it. Just as anyone can learn to bowl, so can anyone learn to be accurate. It simply involves getting the hang of how to roll and aim the ball so that it comes up with the best pinfall.

Roll and *aim:* They are the basics of bowling. As such, they are to get all our attention in this and the next chapter.

To roll the ball correctly requires that you perform three actions in the best manner possible. They are (1) *stance* and *approach;* (2) *release* of the ball; and (3) *follow-through* after release.

Stance is the position taken as you stand ready to roll the ball. Approach is the term for the steps needed to carry you forward as you swing the ball in the pendulum movement that will send it to the pins. Release, of course, refers to that split second when you turn the ball loose. Follow-through is the movement of your arm and body after the ball has left your hand.

STANCE AND APPROACH

All expert bowlers do not use the same approach. Each has his own preference, though most seem to favor what is called the *four-step* approach, so named because of the number of steps that it needs to carry the player forward through his armswing.

Rare is the bowling instructor who does not advise the four-step approach for beginners. It is quite easy to learn, for the number of its steps corresponds exactly with the full pendulum swing of your arm. Other approaches cause you to hurry or delay your swing, but with the four-step, you begin the swing on your very first step and, in a most natural manner, complete it at the exact moment when the final step brings you to the release of the ball. Though you may turn to some other style at a later date, you should certainly start with the four-step. It is the one to which we will give all our attention in this chapter.

When using the four-step approach, you must position yourself—that is, take up your stance—at a point in the approach area that will give you room enough to complete four natural walking steps and then a short slide before you release the ball right at the foul line. If you do not give yourself sufficient distance, you will end up with your feet out in the lane, with the result that your pinfall will not be scored. But, if you start too far back, you will turn the ball loose too soon, and valuable momentum will be lost by the time it reaches the pins. Your first job, then, is to locate the exact spot at which to take up your stance.

It can be found easily. Just walk out to the foul line and turn your back to the pins. Then take four and a half steps into the approach area. Do not stride, but just walk naturally. The four steps cover the ground that you will need for the return trip, and the half step takes up the space necessary for your slide.

Now turn around and face the lane. Check your feet to see exactly where you are standing. You are at what is called your *point of origin*. It is here, exactly this far behind the foul line, that you should stand every time you are ready to bowl, regardless of the lane you are using and regardless of whether you are going for strikes or spares.

Now check the two rows of dots in the approach area; we mentioned them in Chapter 2, and now you can put them to use for the first time. They are lined up on the range finders out in the lane and on the distant pins, with one row located fifteen feet back from the foul line, and the other twelve feet back. Choose the row nearest you and line your feet up on its center dot, placing your left foot just to the right of the dot if you are a right-hander (vice versa if you are a left-hander). Thus positioned, you will have what is called the 1-3 pocket (the space between the No. 1 and No. 3 pins) lying straight ahead if you are a right-hander. If you are a left-hander, you will be looking at the 1-2 pocket.

Many beginners think that they should aim directly at the headpin, but such is not the case. Depending on the hand with which you bowl, your best bet is the 1-3 or the 1-2 pocket. Each has been proved through long experience to be the target that promises the best pin mix and the greatest chance of a strike.

Your job as a beginner is now to roll the ball straight down the lane to the pins. Later, you will want to roll something other than a straight ball and will likely develop the hook ball that you've undoubtedly heard about from other bowlers. And, later, you will get the hang of using other dots for lining yourself up on target. But, for now, do not concern yourself with such matters. Be content with the center dot and with the ball rolled straight ahead. The whole idea is first to develop a solid approach style.

Stance

Having found the point of origin, you are now ready to take up your stance. There are many personal variations in stance, but all are based on three basic types. You may choose to stand perfectly erect, slightly bent forward, or bent far forward so that you are in a half crouch, with your knees bent and "sinking" forward.

In time, you will decide which of the three stances is best suited for you and will make it your own, characterizing it with little variations that you find comfortable and effective. The slight bend, however, is recommended for most beginners and for all of average height. The erect position seems to work best for players who are below average height, while the half crouch is used mostly by exceptionally tall bowlers, for it helps them bring the ball closer to the floor as they complete their arm-swing.

Regardless of your type of stance, you must keep several points in mind as you prepare for your roll.

First, hold the ball a few inches in front of you, make yourself comfortable, and relax; if you wish, you may help yourself relax by bending your knees a little. Set your shoulders so that they are parallel to the foul line, and your feet so that they are aimed directly at the pins; if the feet or shoulders are allowed to angle off to one side, that is the direction in which the ball will travel. Place your feet comfortably apart, with one foot slightly ahead of the other—your left foot if you are a right-hander, your right one if you are a left-hander. For your arm-swing to be natural and fit in with the number of steps in the approach, you must take your first step with the foot on your bowling side. You make it difficult to do otherwise when you place the opposite foot forward.

Second, though you may hold the ball at any height that is comfortable—from knee level to the chin—it should always be positioned slightly toward your bowling side. This will reduce the distance needed to bring it out and down alongside you during your armswing. It will help conserve your strength and add to the ease of your swing.

Third, hold the ball with *both* hands. Place the hand opposite your bowling side under the ball and let it carry most of the weight. Here again, you are conserving your strength. Need it be said that the less tired your bowling hand, the greater your accuracy?

Incidentally, develop the habit of *always* handling the ball with both hands whenever you are not actually executing your armswing. Always pick it up from the return rack with both hands, taking care to keep the backs of your hands toward the outside rims of the track so that your fingers will not be injured by any newly arriving balls from the pit. Do not insert your fingers into the fingerholes and then wrench the ball upward from the track. Do not carry the ball at the end of one hand as you walk to your point of origin, and do not hold it upthrust on your shoulder. All this slowly but surely wears away the strength in your bowling hand.

Next, check the positions of your hands and arms. Your offside hand, of course, should be under the ball and supporting most of the weight. Your bowling hand should be so placed that, were the face of a clock to be drawn on the ball, your thumb would be pointing to eleven o'clock. Your forearm should be straight, so straight that a direct line could be drawn from the back of your hand to your elbow. To assist in get-

ting the straightness, tuck your elbow in close to your side. The straightness is absolutely necessary because, in the next moment, your arm is going to become a pendulum for the swing and, as such, must be as rodlike as the pendulum on an old-fashioned clock. If you bend your wrist or shove your elbow outward, you will "break" the pendulum. The momentum of your roll will be weakened, and your ball will likely roll off target.

Finally, make certain that your fingers are properly placed in the fingerholes. As a beginner, you should grasp the ball in what is known as the *conventional grip*. Your thumb should be inserted to its full length and your fingers to their middle joints. Unless you have your own bowling ball, you will be forced to use this grip, for all house balls are spaced and drilled with it in mind.

When you have grown more expert and have a ball of your own, you may wish to experiment with the more advanced *full fingertip* and *semifingertip* grips, either of which is used by practically all professional bowlers. We will talk about them in a later chapter.

The Approach: The First Step

As you now step through your approach, you want to execute an easy pendulum swing—with the accent on *easy*. For best results, the swing must be natural and smooth throughout. Do not hurry it along or power it in an effort to send the ball on its way with extra speed.

Speed is always desirable, yes, but remember that too much speed will crash the ball through the pins so fast that they will not have the chance for a good mix. The best speed is medium speed. A smooth and easy pendulum swing will get it for you.

The first step in your approach is perhaps the most important of the four, for it involves the start of the movement called the *pushaway*. A good pushaway is vital because it sets up that needed easy armswing.

To execute the pushaway, have both hands thrust the ball outward and downward from your body as you begin the first step. Plan to extend your bowling arm to its *full length* so that it becomes the rodlike pendulum necessary for the swing. At the end of the pushaway, allow your offside hand to leave the ball and glide away to the side, where it will serve to keep you in balance.

Not only must you thrust the ball outward and downward, but you must also move it sideways to a point away from your hip. This puts the ball on a clear track for the armswing and avoids the painful possibility of having it brush or hit you directly as you carry it back past your leg.

Many a bowler, incidentally, holds the ball not just slightly

to his bowling side during the stance but completely away from his hip. His strategy is to eliminate the extra effort of moving the ball sideways in the pushaway, having instead only to send it forward and downward. It is a technique that, with experience, you may wish to try.

As for the step itself: It should be a short one, really no more than a shuffling half step. It should be taken slowly, easily, and deliberately. Our apologies now to left-handers but for the sake of easy illustration, we are going to have to talk from here on as if you are a right-hander, naming the foot that you will use on each step; if you are a southpaw, please remember to reverse the process and use the opposite foot. With this in mind, the first step is made on the right foot.

The Second Step

Your second step is taken on the left foot and is a somewhat longer one than the first. It begins at about the same time your offside hand leaves the ball and the pushaway is completed. Your arm swings downward during the step and should arrive alongside your knee as the step ends.

You will have the natural tendency to accelerate a little on the second step. Go ahead and do so, but do not permit yourself to build up too much speed. The last thing that you want to do is hurry your swing. Keep it easy and natural.

You will be slightly bent forward as you go into the second step, and you will remain bent throughout the rest of the approach. Bend naturally from the waist, sinking a little lower with each step. And keep your shoulders level. Do not allow the shoulder on your bowling side to "sink" with the weight of the ball. Otherwise, you will throw yourself off balance.

At the end of the step the fingers on your bowling hand should be behind the ball, and your thumb pointing almost straight down. As for your offside hand, do not worry about it once it has left the ball at the end of the pushaway. It will naturally move off to the side and seek out the best position to keep you in balance.

The Third Step

On the third step, taken on your right foot, the ball arcs up behind you in the backswing. It should rise to the end of the swing and then start down again by the time the step ends.

Continue to keep your arm arrow-straight and your eye on the target during the backswing. Again, do not try to speed things up; just let the ball weight set the speed. In particular, avoid arcing your arm high as you end the swing. For most

bowlers, the ball should *peak at shoulder level.* To press it higher is to endanger the straightness of your arm and threaten your accuracy.

A special point must be made here. If you are a girl, you know that you cannot give your roll the same power as can a heavier and stronger man. Consequently, you may hear that it is a good idea for you to peak the ball above your shoulder so that you can add momentum to your downswing. A number of instructors may advise you to do so, but Judy Audsley, in her book *Bowling for Women,* warns that the high peak will force you to play a "man's game," making you stress power in place of the best bowling tool at your command: accuracy. She advises all women bowlers to concentrate on the conventional peak in their novice days.

The third step itself is a bit longer than the second, but it should be taken at no more hurried a rate.

The Fourth Step

Taken on your left foot, the fourth step is the longest in the approach sequence. It is a combination of step and slide, with

the latter (depending on the player) running from six inches to just over two feet.

During the step, bring the ball through the downswing, keeping your eyes on the target and your shoulders parallel to the foul line. Continue to bend forward, and bend your left knee, which is now out in front of you. Bring yourself as low to the floor as possible.

Take your slide on the ball of your left foot, and let the slide carry your shoe tip to a point about two or three inches from the foul line. To brake the slide and halt it, simply drop your heel to the floor.

As your arm comes through the downswing, your fingers should be behind the ball. At the end of the slide, your arm should be extended out in front of you, with your hand and the ball traveling over the foul line.

THE RELEASE

Quite as important to your game as the approach is the manner in which you release the ball. All instructors agree with Frank Clause when, in his book *How to Win at Bowling*, he writes that you can execute a beautiful approach and still be a "duffer" if you fail to release the ball correctly.

The release occurs just as your sliding foot comes to a halt. The ball leaves your fingers at a point three or four inches beyond the foul line. With the proper release, the ball will be neither dropped nor thrown. It will glide smoothly onto the lane.

At the moment of the release, you should be well forward over your left knee, with your eyes on the target and your head and shoulders held low. Additionally, your shoulders should be parallel to the foul line. And, of course, your wrist must be firm and your bowling arm pendulum-straight.

To insure that you turn the ball loose beyond the foul line, concentrate on extending your bowling arm far out. As the instructors put it, "reach for the pins." The strategy will also prove of help in your upcoming follow-through.

As you free the ball, do not remove your thumb and fingers

simultaneously. The thumb comes away first, followed a split second later by the fingers. Do not pull your thumb and fingers back, but let the ball slide away from them.

Depending on the type of roll you are bowling—straight, hook, or curve—your thumb and fingers will need to be positioned in certain ways at the moment of release. We will discuss these positions fully in the next chapter, but let us say for now that, in all cases, you must lift your two fingers a little just before the ball leaves them; this action imparts spin and direction to the ball. And, in all cases, your hand should be behind the ball or shaded slightly to the right. Never release a ball with the back of your hand to the pins. And avoid ending up with your fingers on top of the ball, for while it may finally reach the pins, it will much too often skid and slide with little or no control.

THE FOLLOW-THROUGH

At release, the ball should be an inch or two above the lane; it will remain aloft for a split second before settling onto the floor. As it moves away from you, lean forward—again, "reaching for the pins"—and allow your arm to flow upward. This postrelease motion is the follow-through.

The follow-through is a completely reflex action, the natural tendency of your arm to continue its swing through to the very end. It is also one of the most important features of your bowling form, contributing much to the accuracy of your roll. If you do anything to thwart or hamper it, you can count on hurting your game.

Many beginning bowlers have trouble understanding the value of a full and smooth follow-through. Why, they ask, is it necessary to worry about it? How can your actions after the ball is on its way have anything to do with how it rolls to the pins?

The fact of the matter is that, while the follow-through is completed after the release, it *begins* while the fingers are still touching the ball. Granted, only a split second then passes before the ball is off and away. But that is quite enough time for it to feel and react to any odd action.

For instance, let's suppose that your follow-through form is very bad and that you whip your arm across your chest rather than let it rise in a natural arc. The motion starts while your hand is still on the ball. Where else can the ball then travel but in the direction of your "whip"?

In the follow-through, your arm may or may not want to break its pendulum straightness at last and bend at the elbow; let it do what it wants. It should travel up to at least shoulder

level, but it may insist on going higher—up to or above the head. Again, let it do as it pleases. Let it do whatever comes naturally—in both cases, that's your best bet.

How about your body position in the follow-through? Your left knee should remain bent, your left foot should be pointing directly at the target, and your shoulders should still be parallel to the foul line. As for your right leg, it should be extended out behind you, with its foot in the air or on the floor—whichever serves more naturally to keep you in balance.

That you lean forward and reach for the pins is a "must" for a good follow-through. The action assists greatly in giving your arm its smooth, flowing motion. You can do much to insure the best reach possible simply by keeping your eyes on the target until the ball arrives there. This will keep your head down, making it all the easier for you to lean far forward.

Though you must do nothing to hamper your follow-through, you may find that some little extra foot or hand motion crops up quite naturally at its close. Many experts end with a kick of the rear foot. Many others flick the hand or give it a little wave. Still others let the arm fly off to the right or the left. All of these actions are fine—just so long as they are natural to you. But you should join with all the experts in not giving way to them until your arm is at or beyond shoulder level. At that time your follow-through is, for all practical purposes, complete.

A WORD ABOUT PRACTICE

We've talked at length about the fundamentals, and you should have a pretty good idea of what needs to be done when you head to your point of origin, all ready to knock down every pin in sight. But there is a great deal of difference between knowing what to do and being able to do it well. If mastery is to come, you must now practice the fundamentals again and again, just as you must in any sport.

You should not wait to practice until you have arrived at the bowling center. It is not necessary to have the ball always in hand, and so you can always go through the actions of the stance, approach, and release at home. Repeat them time and again until you have them down pat. It is a good idea to stand in front of a mirror at times and watch for mistakes. Correct them immediately so that they will have no chance to become habits.

As you practice—both at home and at the lane—keep one aim uppermost in mind. Once you are certain that your movements are correct, try to execute them in exactly the same way on every roll. Along with *accuracy*, the word *consistency* must become a key word in your bowling vocabulary. It is vital to your success.

5. The Fundamentals: To the Pins

A good approach, release, and follow-through set the ball to moving smoothly. Away it glides, whirring pleasantly. But will it now go where you want it to go? Will it hit the pins in the exact right spot for the best mix possible? What can you do to make certain that it will?

These questions bring us to the topics of this chapter: proper *delivery* and *aim*. Both are vital to your game. Without them, though you may look every inch the top professional as you move to the foul line, you will probably want to sit on your score sheet every time a friend wanders past.

DELIVERY

On your first roll in any frame, you must send the ball along a path that carries it into the 1-3 pocket if you are a right-hander, or the 1-2 pocket if you are a left-hander. We've talked about this before but it always bears repeating, for these pockets offer you the best chance of a good pin mix and, consequently, a strike. Your second roll should move the ball on a path to the spot that you judge will best mix the remaining pins.

The path taken on both rolls depends greatly on your delivery—that is, the style of ball you roll. There are four basic deliveries: the *straight ball*, the *hook*, the *curve*, and the *backup*. Each describes a different path, and each is made possible by the way you position your hand and work your wrist and fingers at the time you release the ball.

Though certain of the deliveries are preferred over others by most players, you are free to use any one of the four, of course choosing the one that you find most comfortable and effective. Even while you are yet mastering your approach, you should begin experimenting with the deliveries. As soon as you find the one that seems most suitable, don't hesitate to develop and perfect it. Once you are rolling it consistently, you can count on a great improvement in your score.

Here now is an explanation of each delivery and of what you should do when bowling it. Again, our apologies to left-handers. For the sake of easy illustration, we are going to describe the deliveries from the right-hander's point of view. If you are a southpaw, all you will need do is reverse the process.

The Straight Ball

Thus far, in all your practice, you have been rolling the ball along a perfectly straight line to the pins. This type of delivery is the easiest of the lot, for it does not force you to think about spinning the ball in such a way that it hooks or curves. You've used it as a matter of "first things first." It has freed your mind to put all your concentration on the fundamentals of approach, release, and follow-through.

And, thus far, you have been making your approaches from the center dot in one of the rear dowel lines. It is the most comfortable place for the get-acquainted period, but now it is time for a change. Let's move your point of origin off to the right of the dot, taking care at the same time to remain the same distance back from the foul line as always. The reason for the move is that the straight ball can be delivered more successfully on a diagonal. Take a look at the 1-3 pocket and you'll see why. Doesn't it seem to "widen" when you move even a little distance off center? Too, you now have a better angle for entering the pocket.

How far need you move? You should try your first rolls from just a few boards away. If necessary, move a bit farther along for your next shots. Just keep experimenting until you find the spot that gives the best results.

Now, for the roll itself: As you did in the last chapter, imagine that the face of a clock is superimposed on the ball. In the instant of release, your thumb should be pointing to twelve o'clock, and your fingers to six o'clock. Thus positioned, your thumb will be aimed directly at the target and your fingers will be beneath the ball. The ball will come easily off your palm and head straight for the target.

Let your thumb come away first. Lift your fingers just slightly (so slightly that there is hardly a perceptible lift) as they leave the ball. This will give it an end-over-end rolling action. At no time should you twist or turn your wrist. Hold it steady.

In the follow-through, arc your hand and arm straight up, "reaching" right for the target pocket. Allow your arm to bend at the elbow if that's what it wants to do. Keep your thumb in the twelve-o'clock position throughout the follow-through.

And that's all there is to it.

The straight ball is an easy, dependable type of delivery, and you may want to stay with it not only in your beginning days but for as long as you bowl. Many a player does—and with great success. But it is more than likely that you will be lured to the hook ball, for you will undoubtedly hear that it is the mainstay of bowling. Indeed, it is exactly *that,* and is the choice of countless top amateurs and professionals. The reason it is so admired is that it creates far more pin action than any other delivery and so promises the best mixes.

The Hook

When you deliver the hook, you impart a sidespin to the ball. The ball travels in a straight line for about three quarters of the distance to the pins, at which point the sidespin curves it inward and drives it into the 1-3 pocket.

Any ball is apt to be deflected when it hits the pins. The joy of the hook ball is that its sidespin reduces deflection to a minimum and so earns the better mix. Instead of being flicked off to the side upon collision, the ball continues plowing through the pins.

The hook is not rolled on a diagonal, and so back you go to the center dot, at least for the time being. Your ball is now lined up on the 1-3 pocket, but whether you will stay where you are depends on the kind of hook you will roll. So much of how the ball hooks is determined by your natural release and the speed of your roll, with faster moving balls tending to arc less sharply. If you find that yours hooks too sharply and curves in ahead of the 1-3 pocket, start moving to the right for your next tries. Soon, you will find just the right starting point.

For the roll, again visualize the face of a clock superimposed on the ball. At release, your thumb should be pointing to ten or eleven o'clock, and your two fingers should be slightly on the right side of the ball. Bowlers have a simpler way of explaining the position. Just reach forward as if "shaking hands" with the pins, they say. It's a perfect description.

As usual, your thumb is away first, followed in a split second by your fingers. While still touching the ball, your fingers will

rise—or lift—to the follow-through. Lift them sharply and, at the same time, move them slightly counterclockwise. Positioned as they are on the side of the ball, they will thus set it to spinning counterclockwise. This is the sidespin that causes the eventual curve inward. To help matters along, there will be a slight and natural counterclockwise turn of the wrist at release.

The lift is all-important to the hook, so execute it sharply and firmly. With good lift, you will get all the spin needed to curve the ball and send it through the pins with little or no deflection. Without good lift, the ball will be quite lifeless.

On the other hand, don't overdo things. Even though you know your wrist is going to turn slightly and naturally at release, keep it firm and straight. Do not try to help matters along by deliberately flipping it counterclockwise. You will do nothing but cause trouble. Let it work naturally.

In the follow-through, reach for the pins as usual. Your arm, because of the counterclockwise lift of your fingers and turn of your wrist, will tend to rise in front of your face. Your hand should end up at about eye level.

The Curve

Many bowlers describe the curve as nothing more than a hook ball with a highly exaggerated arc to it. With this delivery, the ball runs far out to the right side of the lane and then bends back into the 1-3 pocket.

For the roll, you should position yourself with your right foot alongside the center dot. Make your approach on a slight diagonal so that you send the ball angling far right before the inward bend. Your thumb should be pointing to ten o'clock at release, and your fingers should be more to the right side of the ball than for the hook. Lift your fingers sharply and counterclockwise, and let your wrist perform its natural counterclockwise turn.

Positioned far to the right of the ball as they are, your fingers impart more sidespin than with the hook and thus account for the wide, curving action. As with the hook, the sidespin reduces deflection and sends the ball efficiently through the pins.

Should you make this delivery your chief roll, you will soon learn how much curve you naturally give the ball. Depending on the amount of curve, you should aim at the No. 6 or No. 10 pin. If the ball performs as expected, it will then drop into the 1-3 pocket.

Though the curve may come naturally to you, it is not advised for most bowlers, for it is tiring to roll and difficult to control. It was most popular in the prelacquer days when lanes were coated with shellac and required a player to use great force if he hoped to keep the ball from veering off course.

The Backup

The backup ball is also not advised for most, if not practically all, players. In fact, instructors customarily look on it as a sign of weakness in a bowler's style and urge that whatever is causing it be corrected immediately. They describe it as a faulty, erratic delivery that will keep scores low for as long as it is used.

We mention it here just to get it on the record and because you may be one of those very rare players who can handle it. If so, it may prove advantageous to your game.

The backup is a reverse curve. The ball moves far to the left of the lane and then arcs inward, making the 1-2 pocket rather than the 1-3 pocket its primary target. The ball is released from just slightly left of center, with your thumb pointing to one o'clock and your fingers under and slightly on the left side of the ball. At release, you give your wrist a slight *clockwise* turn, imparting a sidespin that is the opposite of that of the hook and curve. Your hand rises to the right in the follow-through.

If you find yourself rolling the backup in your beginning days, when you are really trying for another kind of delivery,

look immediately to your wrist as the probable cause of the trouble. Return to the straight ball and practice keeping your wrist and forearm in a perfectly straight line throughout the delivery. Concentrate on not letting the wrist "break" in a clockwise movement. Once you have mastered the straight ball, you can then begin to experiment with the natural wrist movement involved in the hook and curve.

If you are a girl, you especially need to be on guard against the backup. Thanks to the positioning of one of the muscles in your forearm, the tendency to impart the backup's clockwise spin will be quite strong. To overcome the tendency, concentrate first on keeping the wrist and forearm straight with the straight ball. Then, when you advance to the hook, keep that "shake hands" release position firmly in mind.

AIMING

Along with a good approach, release, and follow-through, a ball that traces a consistent path time and again to the pins is certainly going to improve your game. But it isn't going to do the whole job for you. It needs also to be aimed—and aimed carefully and properly.

Aiming in bowling is not a hit-or-miss proposition. You do not just step up, squint at the distant pins, and then hope for the best. Rather, you have at hand three distinct aiming systems to help you—systems that have been carefully developed over the years and that have proved themselves invaluable. Right from your first day on a lane, you should know what they are.

The three systems are *pin bowling, spot bowling,* and *line bowling.* You will assuredly need to develop and perfect at least one. Or, as do many bowlers, you may want to become accomplished in two or all three, using different of their number for different pin situations.

Pin Bowling

As its name suggests, pin bowling is the system by which you aim the ball at the pins themselves. On your first roll, you concentrate on the 1-3 pocket. On your second, you target in on certain pins or on the best pocket available. All the while, you need pay no attention to the range finders and the dowels out in the lane. They are used primarily in the other systems.

Most beginners use the pin bowling system because it is the most natural of the three. In fact, its use is almost instinctive. With it, you do exactly what you have done all your life when sighting in on any object, regardless of whether you intend to hit it with a stone, a ball, a dart, or an arrow. You look right at the target. Too, the system is meant for the straight ball and is quite easy to master.

Now let's give it a try. Once you have taken your starting position, look down the lane and draw an imaginary line from the foul line to the target. This is the path that your ball will follow when rolled. Next, pick out a spot directly in the front line to mark the beginning of the imaginary line. It is here that the ball is to be released.

You may want to identify the beginning mark by setting it on one of the lane boards. The boards generally vary in pattern and shade, and so make it easy for you to isolate and remember one. You may choose a board by itself or in conjunction with one of the foul-line dots, lane dowels, or range finders—whichever serves you best.

Once you have drawn the imaginary line and marked its beginning, keep it in mind, but shift your eyes back to the target. Keep them there throughout the approach and delivery. Release the ball at the beginning of the imaginary line. If delivered properly, it will roll straight to the target.

Spot Bowling

In bowling, your target is always no less than sixty feet away. This is a goodly distance, one that can cause you to squint hard as you sight in on the pins. As any marksman will tell you, the closer an object is, the easier it is to hit. Spot bowling, which may be used with any type of delivery, is the aiming system that tries to bring the target as close to you as possible.

It does this by having you aim not at the pins themselves. Rather, you select a nearby spot in the lane and line it up on the pins, after which you target in on the spot and roll the ball over it. If you so wish, you may choose two spots—one at the foul line and one out in the lane. The ball is then rolled along an imaginary line connecting the two.

The possible lane spots are many. Some bowlers use one of the range finders. Others use the lane dowels. Many prefer the point where the maple boards join the pine boards. Still others pick out some shaded or patterned spot in a board. It's all a matter of personal preference. Just keep two bits of advice in mind. It is best to keep the spot as near as possible, preferably between ten and sixteen feet out from the foul line. And, if you roll a hook or a curve, make certain that the spot is close enough so that the ball will roll over it and be well away before bending in to the target.

When you make your approach, you should not look at the pins. Keep your eyes on your "spot" and hold them there until the ball has passed over it. If you use the "two spot" method, concentrate first on the foul-line spot. Then, as the ball is released, lift your eyes to the one out in the lane.

Once you have learned to spot bowl, you will, of course, want to use the same spot for every first roll and so give your game consistency. For second rolls, you will need to pick other spots. All will depend on which pins are left standing.

Line Bowling

Line bowling combines spot bowling with pin bowling. With this system, you pick out a series of "checkpoints" along the lane, draw an imaginary line from point to point, and then roll the ball along that line.

Practically all line bowlers use only two or three checkpoints. Those preferring two draw their imaginary line from a spot in the lane to the target pocket. Those who like three add a spot at the foul line.

Your gaze shifts from point to point as you bowl. If you use the "three point" method, you should keep your eye on the foul-line point as you make your approach, moving on to the lane spot once you release the ball. As soon as the ball rolls over the lane spot, you look to the target pocket.

The same applies for two markers, except that you now sight on the lane spot during the approach and then shift to the target pocket after release. Incidentally, there is nothing wrong with reversing the procedure if you find it comfortable and natural to do so. Many expert bowlers prefer to target on the pocket during the approach and then, as the ball is rolling, look to the lane spot.

Of the three aiming systems, spot bowling is said by instructors to be the best. Although many a star performer either pin or line bowls, the spot system promises the greatest accuracy and can be used with any type of delivery.

Because you are rolling a straight ball in your first days, you will undoubtedly pin bowl to aim. But think about experimenting with spot bowling very soon, certainly as soon as you have the fundamentals of the game down pat.

Once you have mastered it, it will serve you well.

6. Solving First Problems

As does every sport, bowling holds its problems for the player. So many little things can—and do—go wrong at any point in the game. Unwanted though they may be, problems are to be expected. For, after all, what you are doing is asking your body to perform up to certain standards and your mind to remember a host of details. Sometimes, each finds it a little difficult to do so.

When first bowling, you may expect to encounter a number of problems that trouble practically every newcomer. Fortunately, all can be solved with practice, and none should be allowed to develop into bad habits. So that you can take care of them immediately, we are going to spend this chapter looking at the most common of their number and making suggestions as to how they can be corrected or avoided altogether.

WRONG STANCE

Does your ball insist on angling off target? Does it even roll so far over that it drops into the gutter with that deadly "clunk" that, so it seems, can be heard from one end of the center to the other?

Perhaps the trouble can be traced to your stance. Are your feet pointed right at your target? If not, you're in difficulty. Even the best-rolled ball in the world will go astray. Whatever direction your feet are pointing—that is the direction the ball will travel.

Often, when your stance has been wrong, you will become conscious that you are angling off target during the approach. You will then try to adjust your armswing at the last second in an attempt to "steer" the ball in the proper direction. This, of course, will harm your swing, your release, and the roll of the ball.

To avoid all these headaches, simply always doublecheck to see that your feet are aimed at the target and that your shoulders are parallel to it.

BENT WRIST

Here is one of the most common beginner problems: the wrist that is bent while the ball is being held in the stance. The bend makes it difficult, if not impossible, for you to turn your arm into the rodlike pendulum necessary for a good swing.

Remember: Your wrist should be firm and straight throughout the stance. You should always be able to draw a straight line from the back of your hand to your elbow. With the "wrist break," as it is called, you can count on losing control of the ball and depriving your roll of accuracy.

THE "UP" PUSHAWAY

Many beginners push the ball *up* and away from their bodies as they begin the pushaway. They think it is the natural thing to do, for it seems to promise a longer and more powerful armswing.

Actually, the "up" movement is of no help at all. It is wasted effort that tires you and harms your timing. It can put your armswing a little behind your steps, thus causing you to hurry it in an effort to catch up.

In the pushaway, the ball should always go *out, down,* and *to the side* of your body. At the end of the pushaway, your arm should be extended to its full pendulum length.

FAULTY ARMSWING

Several faults can crop up in any new bowler's armswing—and then return to haunt him from time to time even after he has become a star performer. One of the most common of the lot is "sidewheeling."

Sidewheeling is caused when you allow yourself to twist sideways to the target and so bring the ball in behind your body on the backswing. Your downward swing is then turned into a sideways arc that ends with your elbow helplessly out

and away from your body at release. Too, at release, your fingers are where they never should be: on top of the ball.

The fault can be corrected by carefully practicing a proper armswing and by concentrating all the while on keeping your shoulders parallel to your target.

The exact opposite of sidewheeling is "sidearming." Here, the arm arcs out from your side on the backswing, causing it then to angle across the front of your body when it comes forward. The result: Your ball is sent off target, or you are

forced to turn your hand at release in an effort to put it on its proper course. In either case, you're in trouble.

Again, the fault is corrected by carefully practicing your armswing, first making certain that your elbow is always held close to your side in the stance. To check that the armswing is correctly executed, you might try practicing with a folded towel tucked under your armpit. If the towel drops to the floor during the swing, you know that you are sidearming.

DRIFTING

"Drifting" is the tendency to walk not in a straight path to the foul line, but to wander slightly to the right or left.

The problem, particularly if you are a lightweight bowler, is sometimes caused by the weight of the ball; it seems literally to "pull" you off course. Too, ball weight can cause you to drop the shoulder on your bowling side. The lowered shoulder will, in its turn, cause you to drift in the first place or will worsen the problem if you already have it.

Concentration and a few practice sessions should easily correct any drift. Concentrate on keeping your shoulders level with each other and parallel to the target. Practice your approach along a single board in the approach area, making certain that you strike it on your first and third steps. You can go on practicing at home by putting down a strip of tape in the hallway or elsewhere.

JAMMING AND DUMPING

When you "jam" the ball, you lay it on the floor and release it behind the foul line. What happens here is that you allow your body to get "in front" of your armswing. You are still bringing the ball through its forward arc as you take your fourth-step slide and lower yourself for the release. The ball cannot help but hit the floor long before it should.

Poor timing is the villain in the jam. You can correct matters simply by slowing your approach.

You may find that you sometimes drop—or "dump"—the

ball behind the foul line. This is altogether different from jamming and usually means that the ball is too heavy for you or that its fingerholes are too large.

RUSHING THE FOUL LINE

Many a jam is caused by "rushing the foul line." Even if you manage to get the ball out over the foul line at release, your hurry will damage your swing and your accuracy.

Until repeated practice acquaints you with what an easy

pendulum swing feels like, you may rush the foul line without being aware of what you are doing. And, even after you have become an experienced player, you may still unwittingly do so in the urgency of competition. A guaranteed way to protect against rushing is to check your left foot (your right if you are left-handed) after you have finished your roll. If it is pointing straight to your target, all is well. But if it is turned inward, you need to take care.

Rushing can be cured in only one way: Consciously slow your approach. Take each of your steps more deliberately.

OFF BALANCE

No one needs to explain what happens to accuracy when a player is off balance. We've all seen the football pass and the baseball or basketball toss go astray when the player is forced to throw it from some haphazard position.

In bowling—and with the same unhappy results—there are a number of ways in which you can be off balance as you slide and release the ball. For instance, as shown in the illustration, you can "rear back"—that is, keep your body straight and so

make it impossible for you to release the ball low to the floor without going off balance. Or you may lean far out to the side and end up doing a clumsy little sideways dance to keep yourself upright after the ball has departed; a little dance or hop after the follow-through is perfectly all right if it's a part of your natural style—but certainly not if it's intended to keep you from going over on your face. Or you may seem to be in fine shape for the release, but still end up wavering uncertainly because the arm opposite your bowling side is not extended out far enough for it to serve as a counterbalance.

The rules for good balance take us back to the fundamentals of release. First, bend far forward at the waist as you slide, and then shift your weight almost entirely to your front foot at release. Bend straight forward and not to the right or left; you can help the direction of the bend by keeping your sliding foot aimed directly at the target. By bending low, you will not only get the ball close to the floor, but will also minimize the pull of its weight and so stabilize your balance.

As for your offside arm, be sure that it flows out to a distance and a height that will make it an effective counterbalance. Ordinarily, it will do so quite naturally. But you may need to give it some attention just to make certain.

LOFTING THE BALL

This is one of the most embarrassing of problems. The ball flies off in an arc and then takes a few thumping bounces along the lane before settling into a roll. The thumps sound like cannon shots, and you're sure that everybody in the center is turning to look at greenhorn you—and that the proprietor is thinking about the level of his lane and sprouting a few new gray hairs.

"Lofting" bothers practically every newcomer at one time or another. It should be overcome as soon as possible, for it can damage not only your score but the equipment. At the core of the problem is timing. Just practice to make certain that you always release the ball only about three or four inches beyond the foul line and an inch or two above the lane floor.

Too, take another look at your body position during the slide and the release. If your knee is bent as it should be and if your body is leaning well forward, you will always deliver the ball low to the floor and be safe from the "loft."

LANE ETIQUETTE

The players above are having no trouble with their bowling styles. But one *does* have a problem with lane etiquette. A basic rule of good conduct in bowling always requires that, when two players are ready to bowl simultaneously, the one on the right is allowed to go first. To bowl along with him is to interfere with his concentration.

Bowlers everywhere play according to a code of good conduct that has been prepared by the American Bowling Congress. Many a newcomer embarrasses himself by breaking some rule of etiquette not because he is impolite but because he simply does not know the code. So that lane etiquette will never be a problem to you, here now are the code rules:

1. Always be ready to take your regular turn promptly. Remember that the player in the lane to your right always has the right-of-way.

2. Take your time in making your delivery, but do not waste time by posing or delaying until everyone else has bowled.

3. Stay on your own approach at all times.

4. After each delivery, return to the back of the approach.

5. Do not use another bowler's ball unless he gives you permission to do so.

6. You may not exactly like your approach area, but do not condition it with resin, chalk, or powder. Other bowlers may prefer it as it is.

7. Concentration is required for good bowling. When your opponent is ready to bowl, courteously allow him to do so without any interference. You will want the same consideration when your turn comes. Save all "kidding" for the bench or the locker room.

8. Though you should be ready to bowl as soon as your turn comes, wait until the pinsetter has completed its cycle and the sweep bar is raised. If you fail to do so, you may damage the machine or the ball.

9. Always respect the equipment. Getting the ball out on the lane is necessary, but avoid lofting, for it damages the lane and the ball—not to mention your score.

10. Always play the game to win, but if you fail to do so, be a gracious loser.

For as long as you bowl, problems are going to crop up in your game. Every player, no matter how masterly and experienced, has to endure his fair share. Some arrive at the most inopportune moments—right in the middle of a tournament, for instance. Some come and go quickly, while others remain to haunt him for days or weeks. Some are quite minor, others quite serious.

Often, you can quickly determine the reason for a sudden and unexpected problem. Perhaps you are tired and your timing is off; perhaps the pressure of competition—the absolute need to strike in a certain frame—causes you to tighten and rush the foul line. At other times, you will be a long while in figuring out what has gone wrong. Perhaps you have unwittingly changed some little something in your style. Perhaps an unsuspected idiosyncrasy has developed in your approach and delivery.

You must react to your particular problems just as every expert reacts to his: Do not let them anger or frustrate you. Do not let them tense you; try to continue rolling a relaxed, confident game. Do not let them interfere with your concentration; lost concentration ends every possibility of a good roll.

Quietly try to assess their cause, asking your friends or the center's instructor for help if necessary. Once you think you have found the cause, make the necessary adjustments.

In a word, treat your problems as a challenge—a challenge that is best met with a level and calm head.

7. Handling Spares

If you are like most new bowlers, you undoubtedly regard the strike as the single most important hit in the game, for it promises the most points for just one roll of the ball. Indeed, it is the game's best point-getter. But it is not the *single* most important bowling hit. Equally important is the spare.

In fact, most expert players think that the spare is even more important. It is the hit that is rolled most often during a game. If you cannot make it work for you, you can never hope for a high tally. But, if you are successful with spares, you will always score well, even though you may roll no more than two or three strikes per game.

Every knowledgeable bowler feels that it is better to be a consistent spare-shooter and an inconsistent strike-getter than to be a player who runs up a respectable string of strikes per game but fails sadly when he comes to sparing.

To develop into a good spare-shooter, you must keep three points in mind:

1. You must be relaxed at all times.
2. You must know the best place to stand when preparing for your delivery.
3. You must know where to aim the ball.

RELAXATION

How can I relax, you may well ask, when faced with a spare? I felt perfectly relaxed on the first roll because I was aiming at a large target. But now I've got one or two pins left standing there far down the lane. They make a much smaller target. It's going to be hard to hit.

The apparent smallness of a target ruins the spare shot for many bowlers, tensing them as it does. Immediately their attitude defeats them; "I'll never be able to hit it" becomes the thought uppermost in their mind. There is absolutely no reason for you to feel the same way.

Why? Because that target of remaining pins is not actually as small as it first seems. Look at it this way:

Suppose that you leave just the 5 pin standing. Granted, it is only about 5 inches wide at its thickest point—but you *do not need to hit it dead-center* to knock it over. A grazing blow on either side will do the job just as well. So you now also have the diameter of the ball (almost 9 inches) working for you. Consequently, your target area jumps to almost 23 inches: 5 inches for the pin and 9 inches to either side for the ball.

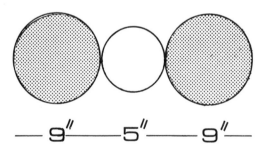

This is quite a sizable target area on a lane that is only 42 inches wide. Actually, it covers more than half the lane width.

Or suppose that the 9 pin is left standing. It is close enough to the gutter so that it is best grazed on one side only. Now your effective target area is about 14 inches across: the diameter of the pin itself plus the diameter of the ball. Still a good-sized target!

So take a positive attitude. Realize that the target is always larger than it looks. Practically every expert bowler will tell you that there is no reason for you to miss any but certain "impossible" spare shots that we will talk about a little later.

Next, do not be annoyed or embarrassed by the pins left standing (they are called a *leave*) at the end of your first roll. Do not think that everyone is looking at you and thinking you are not much of a bowler because you missed a strike or concocted a strange leave. Probably no one is even giving you a glance; everyone is far too interested in his own game for *that,* and the friends who are bowling with you should know enough not to laugh—for they themselves have undoubtedly come up with some pretty odd pinfalls in their time. That sort of thing happens to all bowlers.

So forget who might be looking your way. Relax. Concentrate completely on making your spare.

POSITION

No one can tell you precisely where in the approach area you should stand for spare shots. Your point of origin (the distance back from the foul line) will always be the same, of course, but your exact placement along the width of the approach area will be determined by such factors as comfort, your style of game, the way in which your delivery is behaving at the moment, and the locations of the leaves. In time, experience will show you the best starting points.

There is, however, one basic rule that must be observed whenever positioning yourself for spares, whether you are aiming at a multiple leave or a single pin. Do not take your every shot from a straight-ahead position. Shoot from an angle that will cause the ball to hit the most pins and earn you the best mix. Pick the widest possible angle that seems wise.

Let's see how this rule works for multiple leaves:

1. If your leave is clustered on the left side of the pindeck, you should aim at it from the right half of the approach area.

Leaves that need to be shot from the right side consist of any combination of pins in the group below:

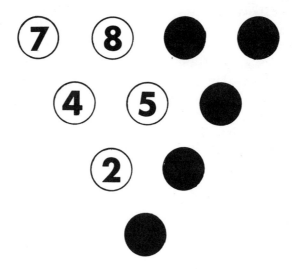

2. If the leave is on the right side of the deck, your roll should come from the left half of the approach area. Those leaves needing to be hit from the left, include any combination of the following pins:

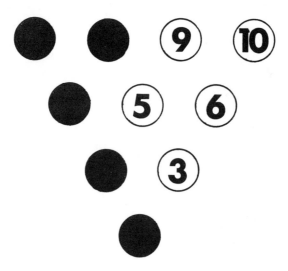

3. If the pins are clustered in and about the center of the deck, you should take aim at the center of the approach—or immediately to either side. Center aim should be taken at any combination of the pins below:

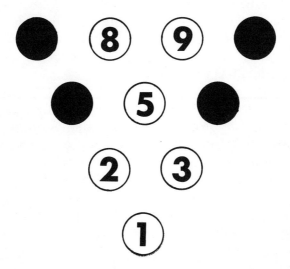

The arrangements of leaves—both single- and multiple-pin—can be many. In fact, the possible combinations have been computed at more than a thousand. And so it is very possible that you will turn up a leave consisting of pins from the center group and one or more of the side groups. In such a case, take your stance at the angle that promises to get the most pins and the best mix.

Now, for single pins: From the illustrations above, you can determine which pins should be hit from right, left, or center; there can be no doubt, for instance, that the 7 pin should be spared from the right. But there are several pins—the 5 and 9 among them—that appear in either two or all three of the illustrations. From which direction should they be spared? So that you will make no aiming mistakes with them—or with any other pin, for that matter—you should learn the following:

1. Aim from the right for pins 2, 4, 7, and 8.
2. Aim from the left for pins 3, 6, and 10.
3. Aim from the center for pins 1, 5, and 9.

Even when you are aiming from the center—for single-pin or multiple leaves—you should give yourself the widest angle that seems wise. For instance, though the 5 and 9 pins are both spared from the center, you will want to stand a little farther to the left for the 9 pin than for the 5.

The same applies, of course, to rolls from the side. Suppose that you have either a 2-8 pin or an 8-pin leave. You will choose one angle on the right of the approach for the 2-8 shot, and a somewhat wider one for the single 8 pin.

The importance of a good angle is perhaps best seen in handling either the 7-pin or the 10-pin leave. Each pin stands at the far corner of the deck, with the gutter just inches from it. If you attempt a roll straight down the lane, you will undoubtedly worry more about sending the ball into the gutter than hitting the pin—and you know what the result will be: Into the gutter the ball is going to tumble! An angle shot across the lane from the opposite corner of the approach area cancels out the problem.

AIMING

Once you have found the proper angle for your roll and prepare to take aim, you should keep several points firmly in mind:

1. As you take your stance, face your target directly. Point your feet at it, and set your shoulders parallel to it. In other words, position yourself exactly as you did for the first roll in the frame—and for the same reason. You want to walk straight toward your target in your approach so that you can execute a pendulum swing that is properly parallel to your body, and not one that causes you to redirect or "steer" the ball at the last moment. Of course, if you rolled your first ball from the center of the approach area, your shoulders were parallel to the foul line; now they will need to be parallel to the pins.

2. Take your position as far behind the foul line as you did for your first roll. This will insure that you have room enough to complete your four steps and slide before reaching the foul line.

3. As a beginner, deliver the same kind of ball for a spare that you did for a strike. If yours was a straight ball on the first roll, use it again. If you rolled a hook, then roll it again. Do not change deliveries—at least, not just yet. For you to switch the type of ball rolled demands that you master two separate styles of delivery. As a novice, you can put yourself in difficulty by doing so. Perfect one delivery at a time.

Once you have mastered both the hook and the straight ball, you may then, depending on the location of the leave, want to use one or the other for your spare. Many expert bowlers do so, with great success. Many others, though they can deliver both with equal skill, like to stay with their hook. It will all be up to you. Experience will show you which way will work best for you.

4. Always take aim so that you include the pin at the head of the leave in your hit. In this way, you will get it to help you topple the pins behind it. For instance, if you have a 1-3 stand, you will have a better chance of making the spare if you hit the 1 pin. If you aim so that you hit only the 3 pin, it can easily miss toppling its companion by flying off to the side or the rear.

5. Always aim the ball to hit as *many* pins as possible. Again, using the 1-3 combination as an example, the ball should drive into the 1-3 pocket so that it strikes both pins. Suppose, however, that you do not go into the pocket but hit the 1 pin on its left side. If struck at a good angle, it may well fly back into the 3 pin. But, if hit at the wrong angle, it can all too easily fly off to the side and leave the 3 pin calmly standing there. The only way to insure the spare is to hit both pins—or, in a bigger leave, as many pins as possible.

6. If you have learned to spot bowl, change your target point out in the lane according to your new position. At first, you may experience a little difficulty in picking out a new point for each type of spare. Time will take care of the problem.

You may either spot or pin bowl for spares. The choice is up to you. Or you may choose to go along with those players who switch from spot to pin bowling on the spare, finding it now advantageous to take direct aim on the pins. Again, it is all up to you. It is recommended, however, that, if you have mastered spot bowling for your strike roll, you continue with it for your spare; it promises greater accuracy in the long run.

Though leaves may come in more than a thousand possible combinations, only about fifty of their number are most often seen. Some of these common leaves are so arranged that the best target spot for clearing away all the pins is obvious. Who needs to be told where to target in on a single pin or on such simple combinations as the 1-3 or 1-2?

Other leaves require some figuring before the best target spot can be selected. You will, of course, want to judge that spot for yourself as each leave comes up in your game, but you will not need to do *all* the figuring. Over the years, bowlers have determined the most effective target areas for all the common leaves. You can make life much easier for yourself by learning what they have found.

There is not space in this book to describe the best target spot for every one of the common leaves. So let us put them into categories and show how each category is best handled, with the advice to be given applying to both right- and left-handers. The diagram below will help you visualize the pins in the various categories as you go along.

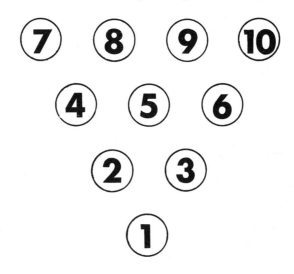

FENCES

Often called "picket fences," these are leaves of three or four pins that angle up one side of the pin setup. On the left side, they are the 1-2-4-7, 1-2-4, and 2-4-7 combinations. Their counterparts on the right side are the 1-3-6-10, 1-3-6, and 3-6-10 combinations.

If your fence is headed by the 1 pin, do not stand at the center of the approach and hope that a square or glancing hit will cause the pin to start a chain reaction. Rather shoot from an angle. If, for instance, your leave is the 1-2-4-7, deliver from the far right and drive the ball through the 1-2 pocket so that it takes out both pins. The toppling 2 pin will then down the 4 pin, and the 4 pin will get the 7 pin.

A common fence problem is the "washout." Here you have a 1-2-4, plus the 10 pin all the way across the deck. Again, shoot from the right and aim to hit the 1 pin a glancing blow on its left side. If all goes well, it will carom across the deck and knock down the 10 pin. The ball will go on to the 2 pin, starting a chain reaction that will attend to the 4 pin.

Apply the same strategy from the opposite side of the lane if you are confronted with the 1-3-6 plus the 7 pin.

Other washouts are the 1-2-10 and 1-3-7 combinations.

SIDE-BY-SIDE LEAVES

As the name suggests, any leave in which two pins are left standing directly alongside each other is a side-by-side leave. Examples of common side-by-siders are the 2-3, 4-5, and 5-6 combinations.

Your job here is to drive the ball between the two pins and let it knock both over. Side-by-side leaves are not especially difficult to handle, but you must take care with your roll, for the space between the inner edges of the pins is about 7¼ inches, while the ball diameter is about 9 inches. The ball is quite wide enough—by about 1¾ inches—to get both pins, but, if it drifts even slightly to one side or the other, you will likely have to settle for just one pin.

A side-by-side leave is rolled just as is any other leave—from the right, left, or center, depending on where it is located. Under no circumstances try to hit one of the pins on its outside edge so that it flies into its neighbor. That is defying the gods of good bowling.

DIAGONAL TWO-PIN LEAVES

Not all two-pin leaves are left standing side by side, of course. Quite a number end up as diagonals—for instance, the 2-5, 3-6, and 6-10 combinations.

Most two-pin diagonals are relatively easy to handle. Depending on their location, you can drive the ball either between or through the two pins.

Certain of their number, however, can fool you. The 6-10 is a good case in point. Especially if you roll a hook ball, you are apt to try hitting the 6 pin only, with the idea of deflecting it back into the 10 pin. Remember, however, that the hook will naturally roll away from this target, and should the ball hook too sharply, it will hit the 6 at such an angle that the pin will fly generally sideways and carom off the lane without touching its neighbor to the rear.

On the 6-10, you are much wiser to stand far to the left of the approach and aim your ball to drive through both pins.

The 4-7 setup, which is located right across the deck from the 6-10, is a little easier to handle with a hook ball, for the hook naturally carries the ball into the 4 rather than away from it. Yet still position yourself at a wide angle and aim to topple both pins with the ball.

On all two-pin diagonals, your best bet is to cover both pins with the ball.

CLUSTERS

The cluster is one of the leaves most often seen. It takes many forms, and can probably best be generally described as

any leave in which several adjacent pins are "clustered" together in one area.

The simplest of the clusters are such three-pin combinations
as the 1-2-3, 2-4-5, or 4-7-8, all of which form small triangles
and are really nothing more than miniatures of the complete
pin setup. More difficult are those that describe staggered lines,
such as the 1-3-5 or the 1-3-5-9. To many bowlers, the greatest
headaches of all are the clusters with "dead wood"—for instance, the simple 2-4-5 triangle with the 8 pin behind it.

You can easily take aim for most of the simple triangle clusters. Just imagine that they are three front pins in the complete setup and bowl as you would for a strike, driving the
ball into the appropriate pocket. Triangle clusters alongside
the gutter—especially the 6-9-10 combination on the right gutter—can be a little more troublesome, however. As in the case
of the single 10-pin leave, do not try to aim straight down the
lane to the 6-9-10. Roll on a diagonal from the far left. You will
have a good pocket for a target.

For the "staggered line" clusters, you must aim for the front
pocket. In the case of four-pin lines—either the 1-3-5-9 or the
1-2-5-8—you will want enough power on the ball to drive it on
through the rear pocket.

When faced with that headachy 2-4-5-8 deadwood problem
(or the "bucket," as it is called), you may try to solve it in one
of two ways.

Some right-handers like to drive the ball into the 2-5 pocket
(2-4 for left-handers), with the ball taking out the first two
pins, and the pins then caroming back to attend to their neighbors. If you hit the pocket at the wrong angle, however, there
is a chance that one or the other of the caroming pins will not
do the work expected of it.

A better bet is to set yourself at an appropriate angle to
the right and aim for the 8 pin. In this way the ball will strike
the 2 pin directly, drive on through the 4-5 pocket (getting
both pins as it goes), and then topple the 8.

The same procedure is used for the 3-5-6-9 combination at
the opposite side of the deck, with the ball, of course, coming
this time from the left of the approach area.

DOUBLE WOOD

Three combinations of pins qualify as double-wood leaves: the 1-5, 2-8, and 5-9. All share one characteristic: One pin stands directly behind the other.

There is only one way to deal with a double-wood leave: Face it as squarely as needs be and have the ball hit the first pin head-on, driving on then to topple the rear pin. Do not try to carom the first pin into the second by hitting it at an angle. The possibility of the pin flying off in any one of a number of wrong directions is great.

A proven way to help a double-wood roll is to take aim on the second pin in line.

The double-wood roll, requiring a perfectly straight delivery to a narrow target, is one of the most difficult in bowling. So take care with it.

SPLITS

A split is a leave in which two or more pins remain standing without any adjacent pins between them. Even the best of bowlers often turn up a split. They know that it usually means trouble on their next roll. And they know that certain splits are absolutely impossible to spare.

The same rules that work for other leaves also work for splits. If the split is on the left of the pindeck, approach it from the right of the approach area. If it is on the right, come in from the left. And if it is in the center, aim from the center.

The easiest splits to convert (though they are not *all that* easy) are the two baby splits: the 2-7 on the left side, and the 3-10 on the right side.

You will have your best chance to spare the 2-7 by positioning yourself on the right side of the lane and aiming into the pocket left by the 4 pin. If properly rolled, the ball will strike the 2 pin a glancing blow on the left side and send it skidding across the lane, with the struck pin deflecting the ball on to the 7.

The 3-10 split should be handled in the same way, but from the left side of the lane.

If you are a right-hander who has learned to deliver a dependable hook, you may wish to hook the ball into the 2 pin at an angle that will knock the pin back against the 7. This is a dangerous shot, though. Anything but a hit at exactly the right angle will deflect the 2 away from the 7.

The wider a split becomes, the more difficult it is to convert. For instance, the 5-10 is difficult, but even more so the wider spaced 3-7. With splits such as these, your only chance is to hit the front pin at an angle that will send it flying back into the rear pin.

The most difficult of all splits are those on a horizontal, the worst being the nightmarish 7-10 combination, with its pins standing the full width of the lane away from each other. Short of a miracle, you will never convert the 7-10 in a lifetime of bowling. You should not even try, but should go for one pin or the other, making sure that you get it and the additional point that it will earn for your score.

Likewise, with such problems as the 4-7 combination with a split 10, do not try to figure some weird angle that will claim all three pins. Go for the sure points. Aim for the 4-7 and leave the 10 in peace.

From your very first days at the lanes, it will be wise for you to watch closely the sort of leaves that come your way. They can tip you off to certain little failings (and big ones) in your game, for they are rarely just accidental. If one or more types of leaves show themselves repeatedly, you may be sure that you are doing something wrong.

For instance, suppose you are rolling a hook and the 9 pin insists on remaining upright. The fault lies with the fact that the ball is hooking too much and not causing pin deflections in the 9's direction.

Other tipoffs to problems:

A constant 4-5 side-by-sider is often caused by too much speed on the roll. The ball is hurrying through too fast for a good mix. Likewise, too little spin can be responsible. Again, a poor mix.

Many splits occur when a ball loses its drive. For example, the ball may enter the 1-3 pocket, but then not drive on to topple the 5 pin and send it flying, with the result that you are left with such splits as the 5-7, 5-10, and 8-10. Loss of drive may result from sidearming or poor timing such as jamming. Too, it may have something to do with lane conditions (more on these conditions in a later chapter).

The 2-4-7 fence customarily results from hitting the headpin a little too squarely. Instead of being deflected on an angle that will start a chain reaction along the fence pins, it flies straight back. On the other hand, the 3-5-9 cluster is probably most often caused by hitting the headpin to the left of its center so that the ball is deflected away from the center of the pin setup.

And, of course, if you leave the headpin standing at any time, you have simply misaimed the ball.

Certainly, many a leave will be accidental. More times than you will care to remember, you will send the ball perfectly into the 1-3 pocket only to have some odd deflections leave you with one or more pins standing. That is all the luck of the game, and every player must live with it. But a constantly repeated leave of any one sort or another is the signal of a flaw somewhere in your delivery. Try immediately to remedy it. With a little thought and care, you will be able to do so.

8. As You Gain Experience

Thus far, we have talked only about the fundamentals of bowling—all those little details of coordination, accuracy, consistency, and concentration that must be mastered before you can ever become a star performer.

Now let us say that you have the fundamentals pretty well in hand. You are perfecting your approach, release, follow-through, and delivery. Your aim is improving daily; more and more, the ball is going where you want it to go—and, on those occasions when it fails to do so, you are beginning to understand *why*. Your scores are steadily on the rise.

It is time to begin talking about more advanced points. They must join the fundamentals to make you the complete and knowledgeable bowler. Some are technical, some are not. Some will enhance your skill. Others will add to your understanding of the game. All will contribute to your enjoyment.

Let's turn to them in this chapter, looking at those that will be of the greatest help as you become a more experienced player. In the next chapter, we'll see those that you will need to know and use if you hope to become a truly expert bowler one day.

Through the years, bowlers have developed a language of their own to describe the various facets of their game quickly and succinctly. The more you bowl and the more players you meet, the more you are going to hear this "language of the lanes." Obviously, you will want to learn it as soon as possible so that you can know what everybody is talking about and so that you can save yourself the red face that always comes of misusing one of its terms.

In the course of this book, we have already met a number of its words: *lane, approach, kegler, strike, spare, miss, split, baby split, fence, bucket, jamming, lofting, sidearming,* and *sidewheeling.* But these are just a few representative terms. There are many more, and you will need a good bit of time to learn them all. Here, to get you started, is a list of the most common bowling terms not mentioned in our preceding chapters.

Anchorman:	The last bowler in a team lineup.
Balk:	Crossing the foul line with the ball but not releasing it.
Bedposts:	The 7-10 split.
Big four:	The 4-6-7-10 split.
Blow:	Failure to make a spare; a miss, an error.
Channel:	The gutter.
Channel ball:	A ball that rolls into the gutter, or channel.
Cherry:	To chop off the front pin by driving it straight back past any other standing pin or pins; an error, a blow.
Chop:	To cherry.
Count:	The number of pins toppled on the first ball, used in figuring a spare score in the previous frame.
Crossover:	A ball that goes into the 1-2 pocket side for a right-hander, or the 1-3 pocket for a left-hander.
Dead wood:	Felled pins that lie on the pindeck after being downed by the first ball in a frame.

Dinner bucket:	Another term for *bucket*—the 2-4-5-8 or 3-5-6-9 leaves.
Double:	Two strikes in succession.
Double pinochle:	The 4-6-7-10 split.
Double 200:	A game of exactly 200 points made by alternate strikes and spares.
Error:	A miss, a blow.
Fast lane:	In many areas of the country, this term refers to a lane whose surface condition keeps a ball from hooking; in other areas, it means a lane that gives the ball too wide a hook. Often, such lanes are described as "holding" or "running" lanes.
Fill:	The number of pins knocked down following a spare.
Goalposts:	Another term for the 7-10 split; *bedposts.*
Gutter ball:	Another term for *channel ball.*
Handicap:	An adjustment of score totals between players or teams to make competition equal.
High board:	A board in the lane that seems to be higher than its companion boards and causes the ball to change course; the term is also used to refer to the low spots in the lane. The high and low spots are caused by board expansions and contractions due to atmospheric conditions.
High hit:	A ball that strikes full on the headpin.
Hole:	The strike pocket—1-3 for right-handers, 1-2 for left-handers.
Kickback:	The side partitions between lanes at the pit end.
Kingpin:	The headpin; in some areas, the 5 pin.
Light hit:	A ball that strikes on the 3-pin side of the 1-3 pocket; also known as a *thin hit.*
Maples:	Nickname for the pins.
Mixer:	A ball that produces a lively action among the pins.
Move in:	To start the approach from or near the center position.

Move out:	To start the approach from or near a corner position.
Nose hit:	A hit full on the headpin; sometimes simply called a *nose*.
Pinching the ball:	Gripping the ball too hard and so causing a poor delivery.
Poison ivy:	The 3-6-10 split.
Railroad:	A split.
Runway:	The approach area.
Scratch:	Bowling based on actual scores and average, and not on handicaps.
Short pin:	A pin that is knocked down, but rolls on the lane without toppling any other pins.
Sleeper:	A pin hidden behind another, such as the 8 and 9 pins in the double wood leaves; in some areas, the leave is known as a *railroad*.
Slow lane:	A lane that either assists or retards a hook ball; its use varies from area to area.
Splice:	The area in the lane where the maple and pine boards are joined; sometimes called the *dovetail*.
Striking out:	Earning three consecutive strikes in the tenth frame.
Tap:	An apparently perfect hit that somehow leaves a pin standing.
Thin hit:	A light hit.
Turkey:	Three strikes in a row.
Woolworth:	The 5-10 split.
Working ball:	A ball that produces good pin action; a *mixer*.

PRACTICE MAKES PERFECT

In Chapter 4, the necessity of practicing the fundamentals was stressed. Practice must now be mentioned again, for it is quite as important to your improving game as it was to your beginning efforts. In fact, it will be vital to your success for as long as you bowl. If you doubt the truth of this, stop by a center and watch a professional or top amateur in the hours or days before a tournament. He doesn't just show up and then sit waiting for the competition to begin. He finds a lane for practice. No matter how talented he is, he always wants to put more polish on his delivery, always wants to be on the lookout for any suddenly appearing problems.

Without practice in your beginning days, you will never get your muscles thoroughly acquainted with or accustomed to the work they must do, nor will you develop the stamina necessary for top bowling. If you give up practicing after you have mastered the fundamentals, you will find that you quickly grow rusty between game sessions. And, without it, you will leave yourself open to all those little flaws that can sneak into even an expert's style and swiftly become an habitual part of it. You will not give yourself a real chance to notice and then correct them.

It is quite easy to practice the fundamentals at home, for, as was said in Chapter 4, you do not need even the ball to help you in getting your approach, release, and follow-through down pat. Nor do you need the ball to practice the lift and counterclockwise turn of the fingers necessary for the hook delivery. Later, you can even practice aiming at home, for there is nothing to stop you from rolling a lightweight ball (even a bowling ball, if you can get your parents to agree) along a carpet and into a target of pillows. Another item often used in at-home practice is an old flatiron or electric iron. Just slide it along the carpet. It works very well in place of the ball.

As at home, your first days on the lane will see you putting all your concentration on the fundamentals. As you improve, start to watch more closely the exact roll of the ball and the behavior of the pins. They will quickly show you where your game needs work. Is your hook too wide—or not wide enough? Do the same types of leaves keep cropping up? Is sparing a problem; do you always miss "clearing" the deck, even on the easiest of leaves? Or do only certain leaves trouble you; are you one of those players who can't seem to convert a single-pin leave even with a ball six feet wide?

Most all problems can be traced to some shortcoming in the fundamentals; there is something wrong somewhere in your approach, your release, your follow-through, your delivery, or your aim. Others, such as the single-pin ogre, can be psychological in origin; you've fooled yourself into thinking that the target is smaller than it actually is and need to remember what was said about actual target size in Chapter 7. No matter what the problem, try to determine its cause and then work to correct it with practice.

When overcoming a particular problem, you will be wise to set aside some of your bowling sessions to work just on it. Do not bother to keep score or even to play a game. Just patiently work on the problem. And work with determination and concentration; a slipshod practice session is of no value. If you have trouble in determining or surmounting the difficulty, bring along a friend who is a more experienced bowler and let him see if he can help. If the center has an instructor, don't be afraid to ask him if he will give you a few minutes of his time.

Not only the physical side of your game may need practice. As in the case of that single-pin leave that you are never able to handle, you may have to work on your attitude. Do you grow too tense in competition? Does one bad roll late in the game "throw" you for the rest of the time? Do you grow angry when you make a mistake? Do you "give up" and literally hand the game to your opponent when you fall behind or run into difficulty? When you need a strike or a spare to stay in the running, do you take your stance and find yourself thinking, "I'll never make it. I'll never make it."?

Any instructor will tell you that attitude is quite as important as physical perfection in bowling. What good does it do to have a faultless style when your mind or your emotions refuse to let it work for you? If you find that some bleak attitude is damaging your game, deliberately replace it with a bright one and then hold that bright one until it becomes a natural part of your thinking. Practice a positive outlook as much as you practice your deliveries. In a surprisingly short time, it will pay amazing dividends.

As soon as you have mastered the basics of bowling—or even before—you may wish for competition keener than that offered by games with your friends.

If so, league play is for you.

Almost without exception, every bowling center features league play for young people. Your center's league may be sponsored by the center itself, but more likely it will be presented under the auspices of the American Junior Bowling Congress or the Youth Bowling Association, both of which are national organizations. In all cases, you may be assured that it will operate according to precise rules of play and conduct, and will be supervised and coached by adult and older teen-age volunteers. Customarily, play is held on Saturdays, though your center may also schedule activities for weekdays after school. Play includes both informal competitions and formal tournaments.

The fact is that you need not wait until you have mastered the fundamentals before joining a league. You are welcome even if you don't know one end of a lane from the other, and you will be taught how to play in the league's teaching program. All leagues put much emphasis on basic instruction, a fact easily seen in the AJBC's way of doing things. It certifies volunteer instructors all across the country, conducts bowling clinics, and makes training films, pamphlets, and a monthly magazine available to its participating groups.

Every league is divided into various subleagues according to player ability, with each subleague consisting of several teams that compete against each other. If you are brand new to the game, you will start on a beginner's subleague team, moving from there to more advanced subleagues as you grow more expert. Ordinarily, you advance on the basis of your scoring average. For instance, once you have attained an average of 90, you may be eligible for the next subleague. You may advance again when your average rises to, say, 110 or 115. And again when you reach 135 or more. Some junior leagues boast of top teams whose player averages stand at 190 or better.

There is usually no charge for instruction in a league. But there is customarily a fee for play in the various competitions and tournaments. Exactly what it is depends much on the center, but you may be assured that it is minimal and will not weigh heavily on your pocketbook, especially when you consider the hours of enjoyment to be had for it. Many young people find that league participation affords them the most inexpensive way of bowling. The fees are usually well below those charged for regular games.

Tournaments are a constant feature of any league program. The AJBC, for example, underwrites a very ambitious tournament awards program and has been known to present as many as three hundred thousand medals, trophies, emblems, and certificates in one year for bowling accomplishment. The awards cover a wide range of competition activities—all the way from highest scores rolled, to success at converting difficult splits. Even the members of the bottom teams receive awards, in recognition of their competitive spirit and their growing improvement. So that all participants have an equal chance at a prize, the many awards are distributed according to age and ability groups.

You may join the AJBC program at your center if you are eighteen years or younger. On graduating from the league, you can move on to the center's adult leagues. Adult leagues are many. Some are intended for men and women; others just for men, and still others exclusively for women. They allow for players of all levels of ability. There is room in them for everyone.

With your center sponsoring league play for all ages, a lifetime of competitive amateur bowling lies ahead of you.

And who knows? You may be one of those many fine players who finally take up the game as a profession.

THE RULES OF THE GAME

Should you decide to join a league, you will need to acquaint yourself thoroughly with all the rules of bowling, most of which apply to specific situations and questions that can arise in team or tournament competition. They are many and there is not space to include them all in this book. So let us simply say here that they are published by the American Bowling Congress and are made available to bowling centers everywhere. As soon as you become a league player, you should ask your center for a copy of the official rule book and then study it closely.

If, on the other hand, you plan only games with your friends, you need know only a few certain basic rules. Should you then run into some unusual situation now and again, the personnel at the center will be happy to explain the regulation governing it. Actually, all that you really need to know for informal play can be summed up in a single statement:

The pins toppled by your ball always count in your score unless (1) a foul is committed, (2) the ball is declared dead, or (3) an illegal pinfall occurs.

A Foul

In earlier chapters, it was said that a foul is committed when your sliding foot crosses the foul line before you are able to release the ball. That foot-that-just-won't-stop-in-time is the most common cause of a foul, but it is certainly not the only one.

The rules of bowling say that a foul occurs when any part of your body touches the foul line itself or goes beyond it to touch any part of the lane, the surrounding bowling equipment, or the building. Suppose that you lose your balance and, though missing the lane floor altogether, stumble onto the covered return track at a point beyond the foul line. Or suppose that, in an attempt to maintain your balance, you nimbly clear the track and land out in the adjoining lane. In both instances, you have committed a foul.

The foul cancels all the pins that are toppled on the roll. Here, in a variety of circumstances, is how the problem is handled:

1. If the foul occurs on your first roll, the fallen pins are reset and you are then permitted to count the number of pins

knocked down on your second roll. If you then topple all the pins, you are credited with a spare rather than a strike.

2. If the foul occurs on your second roll, you are allowed to count only those pins downed on the first roll. You are allowed no further rolls in the frame.

3. In the tenth frame, however, should you foul on the first roll and then topple all the pins on the second roll, you are credited with a spare and allowed to roll again for your final bonus points. If you foul on that roll, then you receive credit only for your spare. No bonus points may be added.

4. If at any time in the game, you foul on both your first and second rolls, you are not credited with any pins.

One point about the foul often confuses new bowlers. They hear the instruction that the ball should come away from the hand at a point about three or four inches beyond the foul line. Since the hand crossed the line, shouldn't a foul be declared?

For a foul to be committed, you must actually touch the foul line or some point beyond it. You are permitted to send your hand or part of your body *above* the foul line without penalty—as indeed you must if you hope for a good release and follow-through.

Dead Ball

Should your ball be declared "dead" on any roll, the pins that it downs will not be counted. Rather, they will be reset and you will be given the opportunity of another roll. The most common circumstances that can cause a ball to be declared dead are:

1. After you have delivered the ball, you immediately see or are told that one or more pins were missing from the pin-deck. You must not wait until later to make your claim of a dead ball.

2. You roll the ball only to see the automatic pinsetter knock down or remove any of the standing pins before the ball reaches its target.

3. As you are making your delivery, another player or a spectator interferes with you.

4. You deliver the ball and see it strike some foreign object out in the lane.

5. You bowl out of turn or in the wrong lane. This rule is usually enforced only in league or tournament play.

Illegal Pinfall

When an illegal pinfall occurs, your roll will be counted in the frame, but the pins that it topples will not be counted. Your pinfall will be declared illegal in any of the following circumstances:

1. You commit a foul.

2. En route to the pins, your ball leaves the lane, but still manages to knock down or move one or more pins.

3. Your ball goes into the pit, hits the rear cushion, and rebounds back onto the deck to knock down one or more pins.

4. A struck pin flies off the deck and then rebounds to a standing position on the deck. (The chances are that you won't mind the loss of a point here, for you will be treated to a once-in-a-lifetime sight.)

5. Any standing pin is toppled during the operation of the pinsetter. The pin must be reset before you can deliver the ball.

With just these few rules in mind, you will be able to bowl informally for many years without argument or misunderstanding. Additionally, to avoid any and all difficulty, you need only apply the general rules of good sense and good sportsmanship. Do not try to settle any dispute over rules with a loud voice; ask for a decision from the center personnel and then accept it gracefully. Do nothing to harm your opponent's game. Do nothing to alter the approach area or the lane in your favor (remember that basic courtesy of not treating the approach area with powder or some other substance). Play to win, but play to win fairly. Win graciously. Lose cheerfully.

9. Becoming a Top Player

By now, you can have no doubt about one fact: Bowling is not the simple game that it may have seemed when you first stood by a lane and watched a masterful player run up an enviable score.

He made it all look so easy that you may have thought, "Anybody can do that." His armswing seemed effortless. There was no frantic lunge but only an unhurried grace in his approach. He set the ball smoothly but firmly on the lane and sent it whirring to the pins at a steady, medium speed. So often did it drive into exactly the right target area that it seemed to be guided by remote control.

You know now that this look of ease is really the look of skill. You know now the coordination, the accuracy, the consistency, and the concentration that lie behind his success. You know that he has mastered completely the fundamentals of bowling.

But his success is not built of fundamentals only. Without them, there can be no success at all, but for there to be great success, they must be joined by other factors. He has learned, for instance, not only how to aim for a strike, but how *best* to aim for it. He knows that there are approaches other than the basic four-step and has perhaps developed one at which he is more adept. He knows that the conventional grip is neither the only nor the best way of holding the ball and has perhaps profited from another. He knows that the lane itself can hinder his game, and he has learned to compensate for the damage it can do.

These and others are factors that you, too, must consider if you now wish to advance to expert status.

THE "BEST" STRIKE

Thus far, we have said that if you hope for a strike, you must drive the ball into the 1-3 pocket (1-2 if you are a left-hander). This is all quite correct, but now that you are on your way to advanced bowling, it is time to talk of *exactly* how the ball should enter that pocket to give you the very best chance for a strike.

Until now, in common with most bowlers, you have probably been aiming the ball directly into the pocket so that it hits the 1 and 3 pins at the same time. And you undoubtedly know the frustrations that can result even when the ball seems to go where you want it to go. Sometimes you will get a strike, and sometimes not.

The problem is that, even though the space between the pins is only about 7¼ inches at its narrowest point, it constitutes a target area a little too wide for aiming a precision hit. If the ball drifts to one side of the pocket or the other— or misses it by a fraction of an inch—it simply will not produce the strike's needed pin action.

You will be wiser to aim at a narrower target. Then, if your ball does drift a bit off course, it will still have a good chance of remaining within an area that will produce fine pin action and perhaps yet earn you a strike. Rather than seeking to pass directly between the 1 and 3 pins, you should take aim on the headpin and plan to hit it a glancing blow.

What you are after, however, is a very precise glancing blow, one that will send the headpin into the 2 pin and so start a chain reaction up the fence. Championship bowler Ed Lubanski, writing in the book *Bowling Secrets of the Pros,* describes the hit this way:

The center of the headpin cuts in half the center board in the lane, namely, the twentieth board. The ball should be rolled so that it hooks in and makes contact while its center is on the seventeenth board—or about three inches to the right of the center of the headpin. Struck at this angle, the headpin will fly back into the 2 pin, starting a chain reaction that will take out the 4 and 7 pins. The ball, still hooking, will attend to the 3 pin, which, in its turn, will topple the 6 and 10 pins.

The ball will then go on to knock down the 5 pin and be deflected into the 9 pin. The 5 pin, for its part, will sail back into the 8 pin, completing the strike.

As you can see, the hit is indeed a precise one. But, since it offers you the best opportunity for a strike, it should be practiced and mastered. In time, along with many an expert bowler, you will be able to handle it successfully more times than not. And remember: Even if the ball drifts slightly, it may still remain in an area that will, with a bit of luck, give you a strike or at least a good pinfall.

While practicing the hit, you must concentrate on both aim and power. Not only must the ball be aimed so that it strikes the headpin correctly, but it also must have the power to drive on through the 3 pin to the 5 pin. If the ball fails to come through with sufficient power, it may be deflected by the 3 pin and miss the 5 altogether or hit it so feebly that the pin will not fly back to take out the 8 pin. On the other hand, if the ball hits the headpin at an incorrect angle, it will then embark on a mistaken course and hit the 5 at angle that will send the pin flying harmlessly off the deck without ever touching the 8. In both cases, you will likely end up without a strike —unless plain good luck intervenes.

Incidentally, as you were reading the definitions in the section on lane language in Chapter 8, you may have wondered why the 5 pin is nicknamed the kingpin in some areas. Now you can see the reason. Unless the 5 is toppled by the ball, there can be no guarantee of a strike.

If you practice the strike hit, you will also profit in another way. In describing the headpin target and how it should be struck, we referred to lane boards by their numbers for the first time in the book. As you now grow more and more expert, you will begin to think more in terms of the board numbers. You will know that the ball must cross a certain board at a certain time to insure hitting a certain target. Or you will know that you want the ball to be on a certain board at the time it makes contact. Practice with the strike hit will be of great help in getting you into the habit of thinking of the boards and their numbers.

THE "SISTER" APPROACHES

Though every instructor advises the four-step approach for the beginner, many advanced bowlers eventually turn to its sisters: the three-step and five-step deliveries. They find one or the other more suitable for their bowling needs, and they see in it certain advantages as to timing, coordination, and momentum. You may be happy with the four-step approach for the rest of your days and so may never give a thought to its sisters, but you will hear them talked about often, and so you should know what they are and what they involve.

Of the two, the five-step approach is by far the better liked. In fact, if you will watch for it on TV tournaments, you will see that it is the choice of a host of top-flight professionals. It may not be as popular as the four-step, but it certainly seems to run it a close second.

Actually, the five-step is nothing more than the four-step approach with an extra, shuffling step added at the start. You take that step with your offside foot (remember, left if you're a right-hander; right if you're left-handed) and do nothing else. The pushaway and the beginning downswing come on the second step, with the ball then reaching the lowest point of the downswing on the third step. It rises to the peak of the backswing and starts down again on the fourth. It continues down and rides forward on the combination step-slide that is the fifth step, after which it heads for the pins.

If you go through the motions of the five-step, you will immediately see that, once you have gotten past the takeoff step, all is as it is in the four-step approach. Your steps and armswing are coordinated in exactly the same way, and your gait will need to be just as slow and deliberate. You will speed up a little, though, on the final three paces.

It is the extra step at the beginning that wins the heart of so many five-step fans. They say that it launches them very smoothly into the approach and thus improves their timing and coordination. In fact, they usually refer to it as their *timing step*. In *How to Win at Bowling*, Frank Clause describes it as being like that helpful waggle of a golf club before the ball is hit.

As for the three-step approach, its supporters say that it gives their arm added momentum by requiring a swift and very strong armswing on the third step. But the fact is that it has precious few supporters these days and, though once quite popular, is now shunned by most professionals. The general feeling is that its demand for speed and power in the armswing makes the risk of loss of control too great for comfort.

You begin the three-step approach on your offside foot, starting the pushaway and downswing immediately. You carry the ball swiftly back to the peak of the downswing on the second step. There is no necessity to "power" the swing at this time in an effort to bring it up to customary shoulder level, for the three-step peak is quite low, usually just a shade above the waist. It is on the third step and slide—a longer slide than usual—that the power really comes into play. You whip the ball down and forward on the slide, with your arm driving it through so that it arrives at the foul line in time for the release.

Though you may one day want to experiment with the five-step approach, it is unlikely that you will ever have much to do with the three-step. Unless it comes very naturally to you, it will prove difficult to perfect and, in addition to spoiling many a game through loss of control, it will end up doing little or nothing for you that the conventional four-step cannot do. If you are a girl or on the lightweight side, don't even bother with it; you really cannot hope for success on that powered downswing unless you've got the kind of arm that usually comes with a football linebacker. And, even if you happen to be the sort who can rip open a shirt sleeve just by flexing a bicep, you should still think twice. The idea of added momentum may be appealing, but remember that it doesn't mean a thing unless it has accuracy working along with it.

If you feel that either the three-step or the five-step comes naturally to you, you will want to experiment with it sooner or later. Go right ahead and do so, for, no matter its short-comings for some, it may turn out to be just right for you. But be sure that you first master the fundamentals of bowling with the always dependable and unbeatable four-step ap-proach.

BALL GRIPS

In Chapter 4, it was advised that, when first bowling, you should hold the ball in the conventional grip. With it, your thumb is inserted to its full length in the thumbhole, and your fingers to their middle joints in the fingerholes. It is an easy, natural grip that can serve you well throughout all your playing days.

But it is not the only grip available. Many expert bowlers eventually turn to one or two others. Both are superior to the conventional grip in that they enable the player to give the ball greater lift and turn in the moment of release. The spin imparted produces an excellent hook that, in its turn, produces an equally excellent pin mix.

The grips are the semifingertip and the full fingertip. If, after hearing each described, you will watch the professionals on televized tournaments, you will see them using one or the other.

With the semifingertip—which is most often simply called the "semi"—the thumb is usually inserted to its full length, while the fingers go in only to a point about midway between the first and second joints. With the full fingertip, the thumb and fingers are inserted only to the first joints.

Both grips, because of the partial insertion of the thumb in one and the partial insertion of the fingers in both, require the player to hold the ball with extra firmness—literally to squeeze it. This "squeeze" assists in producing the more de-cisive lift and turn at the time of release.

As advantageous as the grips are, they are not meant for all players. They are especially not intended for the casual bowler. Both take time to perfect and both require the development of extraordinary finger and wrist strength. Many instructors say that no one should attempt them unless he consistently bowls several times a week, adding that neither women nor young children should bother with them at all. For those of average strength and without too much time for bowling, the conventional grip will serve quite well.

Should you, however, decide to develop either the "semi" or the full fingertip, be prepared for hard work. In your first attempts, you will undoubtedly find the ball difficult, if not impossible, to control. You may even suffer the embarrassment of having it fly out of your hand on the backswing. You will likely also need to use hand and wrist exercises (chief among them the squeezing of a handball daily) to develop the strength necessary for the grip of your choice.

THE ROLLING BALL

Besides hitting the pins in the best target area, the ball should be rolling smoothly if you hope for a good pinfall or, better yet, a strike.

When considering the roll of the ball, you need to keep two points in mind:

First, every ball will skid along the lane for a time before it begins to roll. You should strive to cut this skidding distance to a minimum. Give the ball as much space as possible for its revolutions. The more revolutions it develops, the better will be the pin mix. You can best insure a short skid by lifting your fingers normally at release and then following through smoothly. Don't rush the line and don't try to force extra speed into the roll.

Second, you should have the ball roll in the same way every time it is bowled. This will add to the consistency of your game, and will join with your approach, delivery, and aim in bettering your score.

When bowled, a ball usually rolls in one of three classic ways. It is described accordingly as a *spinner,* a *semispinner,* or a *full roller.*

Any of the three rolls can be identified by a "track" that appears on the surface of the ball after it has been bowled a number of times. This track is formed of dust and "alley dressing," a coating of protective oil that is regularly applied to the lane, usually daily. The track shows itself in different places for each of the rolls.

If the ball is a spinner, you will find the track near the bottom of the ball. If a semispinner, the track will be seen just outside the thumbhole. And if a full roller, the track will circle the ball between the thumbhole and fingerholes.

All three rolls produce a hook ball. The full roller and the semispinner are considered superior to the spinner, and the semispinner is said to be the best of the lot. Most top players strive for it and say that it produces the strongest hook.

The differences in the deliveries of the semispinner and the full roller are seen in the position of the hand and the action of the wrist at the moment of release. For the semispinner, the thumb is pointing to the eleven o'clock position, with the fingers lifting at release, and the wrist turning counterclockwise in the move of the basic hook ball. For the full roller, the thumb points to between ten and eleven o'clock at release. The fingers lift and the wrist turns slightly clockwise. Finally, on the full roller, the wrist is straight as it rises into the follow-through. On the semi, it cocks slightly.

The spinner is not recommended for use, but is mentioned here only so you can recognize it when you see it. At release, the hand is on top of the ball and the wrist is turning counterclockwise. The ball literally spins like a top on the lane, often going out of control. Some bowlers have learned to use the spinner with success (usually moderate success), but many instructors suspect that the player who sticks with it does so because he has been unable to develop the strength necessary for the hook ball's lift and turn.

Though the semispinner is advised over the full roller, either will help you earn a good pin mix. The real point here is consistency. Master one or the other and then, once it is working well for you, deliver it in the same way time and again. The more adept you become, the narrower will be the ball track. The narrowest of tracks is the sign of the best-delivered and smoothest-traveling ball. Some expert players have developed a track that seldom is more than an inch wide.

You need not depend on just the dust-and-alley-dressing track to show you how close you are coming to the roll you want. You can help matters along by fastening a strip of tape to the ball. Let it circle the ball along the desired track, and then watch it turn as the ball moves along the lane.

READING THE LANES

Since all lanes are built to the same specifications and must be level to within 40/1,000 inch, it seems reasonable to think that they all will react to a rolled ball in the same way at all times. But such is not the case, as a few minutes spent bowling on any series of lanes will prove. Each can differ from its neighbors in how it handles a ball. And each can change its characteristics throughout a day of play.

The factors that can influence a lane's way of reacting to a ball are many, but high on any list are atmospheric conditions. If, for instance, you are bowling in low humidity, static electricity may well affect your slide and the roll of the ball by attracting dust and grit to the lane and approach. If the day is hot and humid, the moisture in the lane boards may help your ball hook effectively. But in cold and crisp weather, your hook ball may tend to run in a straighter line.

Chiefly responsible, however, for varying lane conditions is "alley dressing," that thin coat of regularly applied oil that protects the lane by providing a lubrication that keeps the rolling balls from eventually eating through the lacquer finish to the boards themselves. Should you play on a freshly oiled lane, you will likely find your hook ball troublesome; it will tend to skid a goodly distance and so hold back the sidespin necessary for effective hooking action. As time passes, though, and the oil is absorbed into the boards or rolled away by the balls, the lane will alter its personality. Increasingly, your ball will tend to hook more sharply, at last perhaps hooking too much.

When you are learning to bowl, you need not concern yourself with these problems. Your mind will be on other, more basic matters. But as soon as you gain some proficiency, you must become aware of the lane and of what it is doing to your roll. You must, as the experts put it, learn to "read the lane" and then make necessary corrections. Unless you do so, you can only expect a good score when Lady Luck decides to smile in your direction.

While from time to time you may need to work out specific problems, your reading of the lane will usually involve just two questions: Is the lane too "slow"? Or is it too "fast"?

In most parts of the country, a lane is dubbed "slow" when it causes a ball to hook readily or too much. As was said in an earlier chapter, the faster a ball travels, the less it wants to hook, with the lane then getting its name because it tends to retard ball speed. It is also known as a "running lane."

If the ball experiences trouble hooking—or fails to hook altogether—the lane is called "fast." It is sometimes referred to as a "holding lane" (because it literally "holds" back the hook) or a "stiff lane."

Though either lane can cause trouble, most bowlers prefer one that is slightly "slow," liking the assistance that it gives to their hooks. If a lane does nothing to influence a roll adversely, it is called a "natural lane."

In a few areas, the terms "fast" and "slow" are reversed. They then refer not to the reaction of the lane itself but to the action of the ball. Thus, a fast lane becomes one on which the ball hooks "too fast."

Before you ever begin a game, you should deliver several practice rolls for strikes, using them not only to warm up but to check the lane's condition. Roll your usual strike ball. If you spot bowl, aim for your usual strike spot out in the lane. Then watch the ball. If it fails to perform as expected, you have three ways to remedy the situation.

First, you may change your starting position. If you are rolling a hook ball and find it hooking too much, move left for your next delivery. Your new position should take care of the problem by delaying the moment when the ball breaks inward. Of course, continue to bowl over your customary strike spot.

But if the ball fails to hook effectively or at all on your first roll, move to your right. You will now be on a more direct line with the 1-3 pocket. Again, keep your usual strike spot.

You need not move any great distance when adjusting your starting point. Try a shift of just one or two boards at first. If your roll is still off, keep moving farther along until you have found the needed point.

All these directions, naturally, apply if you are a right-hander. As a left-hander, with the 1-2 pocket as your strike target, you will want to reverse the procedure.

What if you roll a straight ball rather than a hook? You will not need to change your starting position. Instead, on a fast lane, simply aim more directly at the headpin. On a slow lane, aim toward the side of the pin.

Now for the other ways of adjusting to the lane: If you are a spot bowler, you may choose to keep your same starting position but alter your strike spot out in the lane. You will need to move the spot to the left on a fast lane and to the right on a slow lane. Once again, do not make the shift a major one. One or two boards will usually be sufficient.

Finally, you may alter the speed of your roll. You will need to deliver the ball more slowly if you are after a greater hooking action, or faster if you want to cut down on the amount of the hook.

Neither of these methods is recommended unless the lane conditions are so bad that they cannot be corrected with a new starting position. Both require an alteration in your basic way of playing, an alteration that can deprive you of all consistency. And an effort to change ball speed demands that you adjust all the hard-won timing in your approach and armswing. It can lead to all sorts of trouble and should be avoided unless there is absolutely no other way to solve your lane problem. Even the most experienced professionals sometimes end up in hot water when they begin toying with ball speed.

Whenever you are experiencing difficulty with your roll, you must, of course, ask yourself if the trouble lies with you or the lane. Your practice rolls should remove all doubt. If you deliver your usual strike ball and it unerringly passes over your strike spot, only to fail in hitting the pins exactly as expected, you can be certain that the lane is at fault.

As was suggested when we were talking about static electricity, the condition of the approach can have an adverse effect on your game. Suppose that a bit of alley dressing has been accidentally dropped there. Should you step in it, you are in for trouble with your slide. You should then ask the center personnel for some steel wool (it is usually kept on hand) with which to clean the bottoms of your shoes. Do not, however, try to solve the problem by sprinkling powder or some other substance on the approach. Remember your bowling etiquette.

Throughout your games, you must keep an eye on the lane's condition. It will change as the hours pass. Remember, a freshly oiled lane will hold the ball from hooking, but all will begin to change as the oil is absorbed or rolled away. You will need to make adjustments accordingly.

Too, you should watch for all the dents, grooves, and tracks that result from the countless balls rolled on the lane between resurfacings. They will show themselves particularly on the right-hander's side, with the left-hander (he numbers only about one in every ten players) blessed with a side that is mirror-smooth and unmarred, truly a tournamentlike sweep of boards. Many of the scars—such as the dents that can edge a ball off course—will interfere with your game. But many others can assist you to a better score; for instance, a track or a series of dents along one stretch of the lane may indicate that the bowlers before you have found that the ball runs better there and so have aimed their rolls accordingly. At times, you may even see that most helpful of aids: a groove worn straight to the pins through constant use. You will see it rarely, though, for the best centers, those sanctioned and inspected by the ABC, never permit their lanes to become deeply grooved or tracked.

10. Bowling's "Little Brothers"

Though tenpins is played everywhere in the United States, it is not the only form of bowling enjoyed by Americans. It has its "little brothers"—several similar games that have long been popular in certain parts of our country. At least three of them can boast of being centuries older than tenpins. All can point to enthusiastic supporters who, while not numbering any-where near tenpins' forty million followers, can certainly count themselves in the thousands.

The principal "little brother" games are lawn bowls, duck-pins, rubberband duckpins, candlepins, and curling. With the exception of curling, all are known as "small ball" games. If you live in an area where one is played and have not yet looked into it, you may be missing out on much pleasurable and challenging competition. So that you can enjoy it along with and as much as tenpins, here now is a get-acquainted sketch of each.

LAWN BOWLS

Lawn bowls—or simply bowls, as it is called elsewhere in the world—is strictly an outdoor game. It has been popular throughout Europe, especially so in England, since the Middle Ages, but can trace its history as far back as ancient Egypt and Greece. In the United States, it is now chiefly found in areas along the eastern seaboard.

Lawn bowls is played on a level stretch of turf known as a bowling green. The over-all green in 120 feet square and is customarily divided into 6 lanes, called *rinks,* with each rink measuring 20 feet wide by 120 feet long. The green is usually surrounded by an earthen terrace about 2 feet high, from which spectators view the action.

The object of the game is to roll a ball closer to a small target ball than does your opponent. The target ball is called a *jack.* It weighs about 10 ounces and may measure not less than 2½ inches in diameter. The bowling ball, which is without finger-holes, is usually made of lignum vitae, a hard tropical wood. It must weigh no more than 3½ pounds and may vary from 4½ to 5½ inches in diameter. It is not a perfectly round ball, but is bulged—or *biased*—slightly on one side, a characteristic that enables the player to impart a curve to the ball's roll.

Lawn bowls may be played between single players or 2-man, 3-man, or 4-man teams. "Teams-of-4" games, as they are called by lawn bowlers, are the ones most often seen. In such games, each team member holds a traditional title. The first man to bowl is the *lead,* and the next 2 are the *second* and *third* players. The fourth man is the *skip* and is the team captain. The positions are not interchangeable in a game.

Each game is divided into *ends,* which are equivalent to frames in tenpins. Action begins when the lead man on one team rolls the target ball at least 75 feet toward the far end of the rink. Then the men on both teams take turns bowling, usually doing so in couples—the leads first, the seconds next, and so on. Depending on how the game is developing, each player calls on one of three strategies. He may try to bowl as close to the jack as possible. He may attempt to place his ball so that it protects that of another teammate. Or he may choose to dislodge a ball that has been well placed by an opponent. All the while, until it is their turn to play, the skips stand near the jack and advise on the bowls to be made.

In all, 16 balls are bowled—2 to a player. Their nearness to the jack is then determined. A point is scored for all bowls closer to the jack than the opposing team's nearest ball. When the count for an end has been made, the jack is again bowled to set up the next target, and play once more begins.

Twenty-one ends decide the game. In single-man competition, the first man to reach 21 points wins. Also, in single-man play, each bowler rolls 4 balls in an end.

DUCKPINS

Duckpins is an American bowling invention, and is now little more than 75 years old. It got its start thanks to two members of baseball's Hall of Fame: John McGraw of the New York Giants and Wilbert Robinson of the Brooklyn Dodgers.

McGraw and Robinson were close friends who together owned a Maryland bowling center in the 1890s. During one summer when tenpin play was slack, several customers took to whiling away the time by rolling a small ball about 5 inches in diameter at the large pins. The pastime promised to be interesting, and it was suggested that the tenpins be taken to a woodworker and trimmed to a size that would better suit the ball.

This McGraw and Robinson did, with the result that a game soon to "catch on" throughout Maryland, the Carolinas, and parts of New England was born. Today, of all bowling's "little brothers," duckpins is the most popular, particularly so in Baltimore and Washington, D.C. League play is prominent wherever the game is found. Duckpins even has its own association to govern play and administer tournaments: the National Duckpin Bowling Congress, whose membership now extends to more than eleven states.

Why the name "duckpins"? Once the tenpins were reduced in size, the ball did not simply knock them down. It sent them flying in all directions—and flying high. McGraw and Robinson, both enthusiastic outdoorsmen, said that the struck pins looked like ducks taking flight. A Baltimore newspaperman soon coined the term "duckpins," and it has belonged to the game ever since.

Until you see the size of the pins and the balls, you will think you are playing on a tenpin lane when you first try duckpins. The lane dimensions are the same, as are the number of pins. The pins are arranged in the traditional triangle, with each in the exact spot it would occupy were it a tenpin. But the pins are "bowling midgets." Each is $9^{13}\!/_{32}$ inches high and $4\frac{1}{8}$ inches across at its widest point; built of rock maple and coated with plastic, it may weigh no more than 1 pound $8\frac{1}{2}$ ounces and no less than 1 pound $7\frac{1}{4}$ ounces. As for the ball, it is made of hard rubber, is without fingerholes, and is about the size of a softball. It must not exceed 5 inches in diameter, and its maximum weight is set at 3 pounds 12 ounces.

Pin and ball sizes make duckpins one of the most exacting of games. Dead accuracy is a "must." First, set as the pins are, the ball can all too easily pass right between them and tumble into the pit without felling a one. Second, when hit, they fly so high that a player often gets little or none of the caroming "chain reaction" so common—and so counted on for success—in tenpins. It is said that duckpin scores of between 120 and 130 are equivalent to 200-plus tallies in tenpins.

Such can be the problems of the game that you are given 3 rolls in a frame. You score a strike if you clear away all the pins on your first roll. All pins down on 2 rolls is a spare. All pins on 3 rolls earns 10 points, but no bonus rolls.

The game is played in 10 frames and is scored exactly as is tenpins, with a strike earning bonus points on the next 2 rolls, and a spare credited with bonus points on the next roll. A 3-step approach is recommended because of the lightweight ball. The best deliveries are the straight and hook ball; the latter is famous for its sharp break, a break that sometimes describes a 45-degree angle. Aiming for spares is taken as in tenpins—from the right, left, or center, depending on the location of the leave. Spot bowling is ill-advised; the equipment is too small and the ball can break too sharply for anything but direct aim on the pins.

If you find accuracy challenging and the mastery of it joyful, then duckpins is the game for you—as is its close relative, rubberband duckpins.

RUBBERBAND DUCKPINS

Rubberband duckpins is an outgrowth of duckpins and, with but 3 differences, is identical to it. The first—and most significant—difference is a strap of hard rubber $1^{13}\!\!/_{64}$ inches wide that is embedded in a slot circling the belly of each pin. Second, the ball, though its maximum diameter is also 5 inches, may weigh no more than 3 pounds 8 ounces. Third, only 2 rolls are permitted in a frame.

All else is the same: The pins number 10 and are set in a triangle; their height is $9^{13}\!\!/_{32}$ inches; 10 frames are played in a game; bonus points on the next roll are awarded for a spare, and on the next 2 rolls for a strike.

The rubber strap not only gives the game its name, but also makes it quite distinct from duckpins. The weight of the rubber keeps the pins from flying so high, and so there is greater mixing action on their part. Strikes and spares become far more common. High averages are not unusual, and perfect games are recorded about as often as in tenpins—hence the 2-rolls-per-frame rule.

The basic instructional tips are the same as those for duckpins. Straight- and hook-ball deliveries are advised, with the novice urged to develop a highly accurate straight ball of medium speed before attempting any other delivery. Again, the three-step approach is recommended because of the lightweight ball. And again, aiming for spares should be taken on as much of a diagonal as possible.

Rubberband duckpins is played chiefly in West Virginia, Ohio, and parts of Pennsylvania. Its greatest following is centered in the Philadelphia area. It is also enjoyed in sections of eastern Canada.

CANDLEPINS

Candlepins, which is played mostly in the New England states and eastern Canada, takes its name from the distinctive shape of its pins. Long and cylindrical, each much resembles a candle, with the exception that each is tapered not at one end, as is the candle, but at both ends. Each stands 15¾ inches high and, at its widest point in the waist, is just under 3 inches.

The ball has the distinction of being the smallest used in any bowling game. Made of hard rubber, it has a maximum diameter of 4½ inches and a maximum weight of 2 pounds 7 ounces. It is one of the most difficult of bowling balls to deliver, for its size and weight tempt the player to throw rather than roll it.

Because of the slender pins, the wide spacing between them (they are set in the very same spots as the fatter ten-pins), and the small ball size, the game allows 3 rolls in a frame, with a game consisting of 10 frames. As in duckpins, all pins cleared away on the first roll is a strike, and in 2 rolls, a spare. The conventional bonus rolls are awarded for strikes and spares.

You may first think that with a spacing of no less than 9 inches between pins, an impossible accuracy is required for candlepin play. Indeed, accuracy is mandatory, but the game includes a feature to help your scoring chances. Fallen pins that remain on the deck within a frame are not swept away. You are entitled to aim at them and let their caroming action assist in removing their still-standing neighbors.

But make no mistake. You cannot simply send the ball into the dead pins and automatically produce a good fall. They must be hit at a proper angle if they are to be of any help. If struck at the wrong angle, they can fly harmlessly off the deck. If clipped at one end or the other, they will likely spin like tops, remaining where they are and not touching a pin nearby. Careful aim is necessary throughout.

Instructional suggestions begin with ball weight and size. Both make it difficult to control the hook and curve, and so most candlepin players stay with the straight ball. A slow and deliberate three-step approach should be used, and the ball, so that it will be rolled rather than thrown, should be released at the moment it swings past the ankle of your sliding foot. Unless you have fallen pins on the deck, you should aim for spares in the customary ways. Otherwise, you should line up your roll so that it will hit a fallen pin or pins at the angle promising the most advantageous caroming action.

A word needs now be said on how the ball should be held. (What is to be said here, incidentally, applies not only to candlepins but to all small-ball games.) Because it is small and without fingerholes, you will be tempted to hold the ball in the palm of your hand, as though it were a softball. Actually, at no time should the ball touch your palm. It should be held by the fingers and the thumb, and should be released just beyond the foul line and as close to the floor as possible. Ideally, it will settle onto the lane about 6 to 12 inches beyond the foul line and will then run smoothly, without bouncing, to the pins.

Likewise, a special word must be said about the score sheet in candlepins. Its line of scoring frames does not run horizontally on the sheet, but vertically. Each frame is divided into 2 equal compartments: one for your growing tally, the other for your scoring marks.

The scoring marks tend to confuse many a tenpin player at first. An X, for instance, does not signal a strike, but rather the fact that all pins have been toppled in 3 rolls. As for the strike, it is marked with two diagonal lines (//). A spare, as usual, is signified with a single diagonal line (/), but the miss is not tagged with a dash. Simply, the number of toppled pins is recorded. Otherwise, scoring is the same as in tenpins.

Candlepins is the outgrowth of an old European game called skittles. As such, it joins lawn bowls in being a much older game than tenpins. In turn, they are joined by the next game to be described: curling.

CURLING

Curling is often called "bowling on ice." Believed to have originated in the Netherlands, it won its first widespread popularity about four hundred years ago in Scotland, where it is still played. It can be found in most countries where the winters are severe, and is much enjoyed in Canada and in several of our northernmost states.

The game's "playing field" is an area of level ice 146 feet long by 14 feet wide. Competing are 2 4-man teams called *rinks.* The players slide heavy, smooth stones toward a circular *house,* a target marked in the ice 126 feet from their starting point. The house consists of 3 circles, the outermost of which is 12 feet in diameter. Within the smallest inner circle is a "bulls-eye," which is called a *tee.* The object of the game is to beat your opponent in sliding the stones close to the tee.

Aside from being round, the stones bear little resemblance to a bowling ball. Those used in the United States and Canada generally weigh 42½ pounds, but weights may range from 40 to 45 pounds elsewhere. Each has a circumference of about 36 inches and is flat on both the top and bottom. Each is equipped with a handle on top.

The team players hold the same titles as in lawn bowls. The first man to bowl is the lead, while the last man is the skip and the team captain. Too, as in lawn bowls, the game is divided into ends. The usual game, however, consists not of 21 ends, but of only 10 or 12.

Each player bowls 2 stones in an end, doing so from a foothold called a *hack.* To bowl, he places the ball of his right foot in the hack and then, with both feet together, he crouches low to grasp the stone, which is placed on the ice to his side and somewhat ahead of him. He grips the stone by its handle, slides the stone straight back, and rises so that he brings it up off the ice at the end of the backswing. When his arm comes forward to release, he turns his palm either up or down, thus imparting a right or left curve to the slide.

It is this action of the hand that gives the game its name. The curve is traditionally called the *curl.*

As in lawn bowls, each player employs one of 3 strategies as he makes his delivery, with his choice determined by how the game is developing. He may try to come close to the tee; he may try to guard his own or a teammate's well-positioned stone with another; or he may attempt to knock away an opponent's too-close-for-comfort placement.

One of the most unusual features in curling is the sweeping that is permitted in the path of the sliding stones. While his teammates bowl, the skip stands near the house, directs the deliveries to be made, and then watches the progress of each sliding stone. If a stone seems to be traveling too slowly or threatens to stop short of its mark, he shouts the command, "Sweep." Two teammates, armed with brooms, then run alongside the stone, clearing its path of any impeding ice or frost.

When all stones have been delivered, their closeness to the tee is judged. Only one team is scored in each end, receiving one point for each stone that is closer to the tee than any of those belonging to the opposition. When play commences again, the stones are sent sliding in the opposite direction.

Curling is recognized as one of the most strenuous of games, and certainly as *the* most strenuous of the bowling games. Played in frigid weather and requiring the delivery of stones weighing more than 40 pounds, it is not for someone who would rather sit home by the fire. But if you are a winter sports enthusiast, you will likely find it a stimulating addition to your list of activities—and the 2 hours usually needed to complete a game may just turn out to be the best you spend on a frosty day.

A Final Note

Many topics have been covered in this book: the history of bowling, the fundamentals necessary for every newcomer to master, the techniques advised for improved and then expert play, and the various bowling games of special appeal to certain parts of the country.

It is hoped that you will profit from them all, and that they will not only help your performance but will also contribute to your lifelong enjoyment of the game.

Only one thing remains to be said:

Good luck and good bowling!

Index

EDWARD F. DOLAN, Jr., was born and educated in California, where he and his family live at present. He has lived in the state most of his life. After serving in the 101st Airborne Division during World War II, he was chairman of the Department of Speech and Drama at Monticello College, Alton, Illinois, for three years. While writing books for young people, he spent seven years as a free-lance writer in radio and television, and was a teacher for some years after that. His first book was published in 1958 and he has averaged a book a year since then, while continuing to do free-lance magazine writing and editorial work. For the past ten years, Mr. Dolan has also owned and operated a small publishing company, which produces school materials for mentally retarded children.